T0143144

"Tales"
From The Tarmac

An astonishing "behind the scenes" anthology of *true* cases about passengers and ground staff at airports worldwide

Claudia Helena Oxee

Order this book online at www.trafford.com
or email orders@trafford.com

Most Trafford titles are also available at major online book retailers.

Printed in the United States of America.

ISBN: 978-1-4269-5034-6 (sc)
ISBN: 978-1-4269-5035-3 (e)

Library of Congress Control Number: 2010917778

Trafford rev. 03/25/2011

 www.trafford.com

North America & international
toll-free: 1 888 232 4444 (USA & Canada)
phone: 250 383 6864 ♦ fax: 812 355 4082

TABLE OF CONTENTS

DEDICATION

The proverbial book dedication is tantamount to personal gratitude for those whose encouragement was a contributing factor to the success of their book. To everyone who has graciously tendered their valuable time and their ubiquitous encounters, and to everyone whose memorable airport experiences have remained enmeshed in our minds forever, I dedicate this book to you, as *you* were the inspiration for Tales From The Tarmac.

I had the privilege of working at JFK in New York for sixteen years. My initiation as a neophyte began with TWA, Iberia, Pan Am and eventually I worked my way up to Station Manager for a fine German Airline, LTU INT'L AIRWAYS. This airline, now known as AIR BERLIN, flew, and still does, to exotic seacoast destinations worldwide from its home base in Dusseldorf, Germany. I relinquished my lucrative job as a full-time fur model in NYC and traded in the furs for a uniform, and the runway for a jetway.

I would like to share some of these tales with you, ranging from heart-throbbing to heart-wrenching, and from the ridiculous to the sublime. In addition to my personal stories, I have prevailed upon endearing friends and colleagues to regale us with some of their stranger than fiction tales. The diversity of passengers also made the experiences unique and as our stories unfold, perhaps you may recognize yourself as one of the cast members!

I must preface the list of accolades by thanking Ursula Goeschen, former LTU Station Manager, who was given my name by a Pan Am VIP who felt I was capable of being her assistant. It was clearly a case of *who* I knew in addition to *what* I knew. During the initial interview, my first impressions of Ursula were intimidating since she was quite attractive, elegantly dressed, coifed, intelligent and unpretentious. She was very straight forward regarding the responsibilities of the job. Fortunately, her impression of me was mirrored and the rest became history. A short time later, Ursula left LTU for a more lucrative career which enabled me to sprout bigger wings and vie for the position as Station Manager.

Because of her good judgment call by hiring me in April of '89, my life was enriched with incredible people who welcomed me to the airline and into the airport family. Among my many privileges, the most rewarding one was hiring and working side by side with my daughter. So kudos to you Dearest Lara, for then ......and now! You make me so proud!

Last but *far* from least, my wonderful and patient husband Jack who admirably championed my literary adventure down memory lane with love! His extensive advertising and marketing skills were most helpful, as was his candid and occasional ambiguous critique.

In essence, I am so humbly grateful to all of you who were destined to share a paralleled path with me, while my JFK journey ran its amazing course.

PREFACE

A multi-faceted *insiders* crash course on the lunacy professional airport ground staff must face on a daily basis.

...what happened to the non-English speaking wheelchair bound senior citizen?

...or the horny halfwit passenger who had malfunctioning dildo issues!

...what would you do with a young child whose parents forgot to pick him up?

...would you know how to handle a severely retarded passenger who was permanently discarded by her family in Europe and sent alone to JFK?

...did you ever have an evening of dining and singing with Pavarotti on your social calendar?

...what about the darling little drunk?

…how did JFK's chick magnet handle thousands of little foreign born babes in sub degree weather?

…then there was beautiful Ireland with oh so many green pastures and red faces!

…gator-aid…it wasn't just a drink in an airport vending machine….it had teeth and an attitude

…gain behind the scene insight to bombings and hijackings while the world watched in horror

…did you know that besides tulips and wooden shoes, the Dutch, via Martinair, provided the U.S. with a fleet of aircraft for coalition troops and supplies during the first Gulf War?

.addictions…not just for druggies…, the airline industry itself is an addiction…

…governments are the downfall or stability of a country. The last several candid stories of the book take place in Iran, a land of peace loving people that has and continues to suffer under their despotic leadership. Judge for yourself!

…these, along with many other crazy "tales" are indicative of the daily nuances that occur worldwide. The only difference is the airport location and the cast of players that make these incredible experiences universal!

GLOSSARY

A/C .... Aircraft

ATA .... Actual Time of Arrival

ATD .... Actual Time of Departure

AFT .... Rear Cabin Section of the Aircraft

ATC .... Air Traffic Control, Ground Based Controllers in the Tower Who Direct Airborne and Ground Aircraft. They Separate Aircrafts to Prevent Collisions By Organizing the Flow of Aircraft Traffic.

AUTO LINK............................ Authorized Vehicle Used
To Transport Passengers
From One Terminal To
Another

BLOCKS/CHOCKS .... Wedges of Sturdy
Material that are Placed
Behind the Wheels of
the Aircraft To Prevent
Accidental Movement
While at the Gate or on
the Tarmac

BUCKET SHOPS .... Consolidators Who Sell
Low Discounted Fares
Where Passengers Fly On
a Stand-By Basis

BULKHEAD........................... Upright Partition/Wall
That Separates Class of
Services and Galleys

COMP.................................... Complimentary

CONTROLLED AIRSPACE .. Air Space in Which Air
Traffic Control has the
Authority to Separate and
Control Air Traffic

DEADHEADING .... On Duty Crew Member
Flying Without Passengers
or Cargo

the Airport in Which
The Final Descent For
Landing Begins.

FUSELAGE .... Central Body of Aircraft

GALLEY.................................. On board Forward, Mid
and Aft Food Preparation
Areas

GATE CHECK .... When Flight Manifest,
Boarding Pass And
Number of Pax Counts
Match

GMC .... Ground Control
Movement, Controllers
Responsible for Active
Taxiways, Tarmacs And
Gate Areas

GPS .... Global Positioning
System, Equipment
Which Enables Pilots to
Determine Their Latitude,
Longitude and Altitude,
Comprised of a Linked
System of 24 Satellites

GOM...................................... Ground Operating
Manual

EOM .... Emergency Operating
Manual

Boarding or Deplaning. They are Manned By Bridge Operators and are Hydraulically Attached to the Door of the Aircraft Upon Arrival and Departure

NO-SHOW .... Passenger Who Does
not Show Up for Their
Booked flight

OUTBOUND .... Flight Leaving Local
Airport

O/B .... On Board

PAX .... Passenger

PLANE MATE .... A 125 Passenger
Hydraulic Vehicle Used in
Transporting Passengers
Via the Tarmac to and
from the Aircraft When a
Gate is Not Available.

PNR .... Passenger Name
Record, All pertinent
Computerized Booking
Information Taken When
Reservation is made by
the Passenger

PORT .... Left Side of Cabin Facing
the Cockpit

PUSHBACK .... Ground Procedure by
Which the Aircraft is
Pushed Backwards,
Away from the Gate
by an External Power
called a Tug. Pushbacks

are Subject to Ground Control Clearance to Facilitate Ground Movement on Taxiways. The Pilot Communicates with the Ground Tug Handler via a Headset that is Connected near the Nose Gear. Once Clearance is Obtained, The Pushback Begins.

PURSER.................................. Chief Flight Attendant

PAYLOAD.............................. Total Carrying Capacity of the Aircraft…Fuel, Cargo etc.,

RAMP .... Tarmac Where Aircrafts Park

QUEUE.................................. Lines of Passengers

REVERSE THRUST .... Used at Touchdown Along with Spoilers to Decelerate Runway Speed

SKY MARSHAL...................... Armed Undercover Law / Security Officer onboard Commercial Aircraft to Counter Hijackings or other Airborne Criminal Actions

SOP .... Standard Operating
Procedures

STARBOARD......................... Right Side of Cabin
Facing the Cockpit

STANDBY.............................. Unconfirmed Seat...
Upon Completion of
Boarding, Passenger is
Advised by Gate Agent
if an Empty Seat is
Available... Also Referred
to as S/A.....Space
Available

STATION MANAGER........... A Person with Levels
of Security Clearance
Authorized by the
Airline and the Airport
To Handle All Aspects
of Flight Operations in
Their Designated city
with Ability to Render
and Execute Prudent
Judgment Calls

TURNAROUND .... Allotted Ground Time by
Air Traffic Control at the
Arriving Airport Before
Returning to Hub

UM.. Unaccompanied Minor
Traveling Without a
Parent or Guardian

UNFORGETTABLE

The summer months at airports are demanding due to the upsurge of passengers (pax's) and rigorous schedules. At times, agents must work several flights simultaneously and are pulled in many directions.

My first JFK job was for TWA in the International Terminal. Training was a mandatory four weeks. As a newbie to the industry, I was a TWA *white jacket* employee, aka, a glorified gofer. My schedule consisted of absolutely no weekends or holidays off and subsequently I felt I'd be going from the airport straight into an old age home due to inhumane work hours. My social life was contingent upon each flight day's events and required major adjustments. Eventually, as acceptance overrode ambiguity, the transition was a bit more tolerable. I was low on the totem pole, both schedule and salary-wise, and for the first few weeks, I experienced an acute level of intimidation. Despite the above, my uniform looked fabulous and I had an attitude that TWA was privileged to have someone like me with thirty eight years of life experience. After all, wisdom comes with age, so I thought!

I was a seasoned traveler, taught middle school for a year in Vienna, Austria, had a lavish NYC lifestyle as a fur model for seven years, raised a wonderful daughter in the face of marital adversities and so on and so forth! In essence, my life experiences to date had been interesting to say the least, yet I was naively altruistic with an "It's a small world after all" mindset! My glass was always half full, yet the insecurities of beginning a new career were overwhelming especially since my former high-paying modeling salary plummeted down several *hundred* dollars per week. That alone was a frightening reality. Then there was the fact that I was working at one of the world's most scrupulous airport's, not as a pax this time, but rather, servicing them.

I often speak about the importance of fulfilling one's dreams in life. Many of mine never came to fruition for reasons beyond my control. Having had a love of aviation, one passion on my wish list was to become a pilot. Unfortunately, my vision since birth was 20/400 in both eyes and the rest is self explanatory. Flying lessons are not given in braille! My eye glasses were tantamount to binoculars and lasik surgery at that time hadn't been developed enough to handle my ocular challenges.

My first day at JFK was awkward as any new job would be. No one made nicey-nice to me, nor was there any vote of confidence from staff. I felt totally invisible and tried to be perky (basically kiss ass) as I was ordered around with not even an interest by any one as to who I was. Go figure!

After training, the day our uniforms were issued, the instructors stressed the importance of wearing practical shoes since comfort must precede vanity. Poppycock to that nonsensical idea! Couldn't they see that I was a walking fashion plate? Practical old-lady orthopedic shoes were not touching my elegant feet! Even though my shoe closet was ridiculously congested, I justified buying a new pair of gorgeous designer *uniform* shoes. After only two hours on the job, both feet had blisters the size of ripe cherry tomatoes. They burned like hell, and were fused to my pantyhose since gofering required walking briskly back and forth many times throughout the terminal. It was painstakingly........ the agony of de-feet!

While passing a gate that was deplaning pax's from an inbound flight, I noticed a little old white-haired wheelchair-bound man. It struck me odd that he had been left unattended. Having been taught that when wheelchair pax's travel alone, an agent must assist them for the duration of their ground time. This Gippetto-esque senior was in transit from Cleveland after visiting family, and returning back home via JFK to his quaint little village in Italy.

The designated MAAS, (meet & assist agent) who took the pax off the aircraft (a/c), positioned the wheelchair in a corner at the gate area near a WC. I assumed that the agent was briefly called away and would return to continue his assignment. A short while later, there sat the pax, still tucked away in the corner, just quietly looking around. He politely smiled and I dismissed any concerns considering that he didn't appear to be in any notable distress. As before, I returned his smile and went on to my next assignment.

The TWA International terminal was extremely chaotic that sweltering summer afternoon. I was pulled from the Paris gate to assist with the Tel Aviv flight since it had a delay and the natives were getting restless, so, off I went to lend a hand with pax damage control. While walking to the assigned gate, peripherally, I saw the man *still* perched by the WC. I was angered by the fact that he hadn't been moved from that spot for well over an hour. I went over to him and realized he spoke only Italian. Softly, he began sobbing and reached up for my hand begging pitifully over and over for help. In my airport Italian, I clutched his trembling hands and assured him I would! After retrieving documents from his front shirt pocket, it was apparent that he was a transiting pax. Due to the negligence of the MAAS agent, his Rome flight had departed two hours prior and no one had bothered to look for him. I knew the Rome gate agents must have had an incorrect gate-check (boarding-pass count must match pax-count), since the man never boarded the a/c. He was alone and completely defenseless. This was also a security breach since his bags had been transferred from the Ohio flight to the Rome flight without him.

In lieu of carrying out my Tel Aviv assignment, I consoled this sweet man and via gentle hand gestures, attempted to calm his anxiety by radioing for assistance. Through his tears, he agonizingly pointed to the WC. Twenty minutes later, a supervisor finally came and displayed annoyance towards *me*. Being my first day, I thought I broke a cardinal TWA bathroom rule by requesting help for this handicapped person. I expressed contempt at the unprofessional attitude of the supervisor of size and took the liberty of chastising the agent's negligence. Thinking it would evoke sympathy from this heartless bitch and that the ineptness of the agent would be acknowledged, she turned her back towards me, called a male agent and told him a wheelchair pax needed assistance. That was it! Then, Miss Congeniality blatantly dismissed me. While the witch was on her radio with other TWA issues, once again via hand gestures, I reassured my buddy that I'd be back. You effing Bitch was my only sentiment as

I walked away under her orders. I was totally perplexed by her calloused behavior. That was my first and unfortunately, not my last encounter with that porker supervisor.

The 747 Tel Aviv flight had just finished boarding. The gate agents were maniacally scrambling around trying to get a successful gate-check so the a/c could leave. My presence was not at all missed. I just stood there like a fool thinking to myself, ok, all these little TWA shits can go suck an egg....I'm done! Eventually I learned the hard way as to why I had been so rudely ignored. Interrupting gate agents while they counted 400 boarding passes in the last chaotic moments before the ETD could have caused a miscount and a delay. Had I distracted them, *OOPS* just wouldn't cut it! *Who knew!*

After the departure, the gate supervisor gave me my next assignment. By then, my oozing blisters were tantamount to firecrackers detonating on my feet, so my next jaunt was to a concession stand to purchase band-aids. I hobbled to the ladies room, slowly peeled off my pantyhose and strategically placed them all over my bloodied sores. Oh, how I desperately craved the ortho shoes instead of the new heels. The pain was analogous to swimming in the salty Dead Sea with open wounds, which I've foolishly done on a few flighty occasions.

Fast forward two hours later and there he *still* sat, *still* near the WC. My heart broke as I approached his wheelchair now for the fourth time. I knelt down to him at eye level out of respect and compassion and held both his hands. His eyes again welled with tears as did mine. Whatever the consequences were at that point, it didn't matter. It was my mission to get him on a flight back home immediately. The adrenaline started flowing and my raw flesh wounds became secondary. First, I wheeled him into the TWA commissary, angrily explained the inhumane experience the pax had been subjected to and a hot meal was on its way. From there, this same kind-hearted TWA agent checked the computer and found a flight leaving that night on Alitalia for Rome with a connection in the morning to his home town. Since I would not let my buddy out of sight, the agent arranged for an autolink transfer for us to the Alitalia terminal. Upon arrival, I carefully wheeled him in, asked for the Station Manager and requested an upgrade considering the horrendous ordeal he had endured.

Josephine T. (rest in peace) was appalled by the incidents and cordially complied. She spoke in Italian and reassured him that while he was airborne, his family would be notified and they'd be at the airport upon his arrival. Under these circumstances, his TWA tickets were accepted at face value.

TWA was a great airline, as were the people I eventually befriended and socialized with many a night in Kew Gardens, N.Y. The ground and flight crews officially dubbed me "Morgana" claiming I was a Morgan Fairchild look-a-like. I graciously accepted. Who was I to argue with smart people! The negligence that the MAAS agent displayed that day was truly *not* the norm. The porker supervisor on the other hand really *was* a pig! We were oil and water from the first magical moments our eyes met.

I insisted on bringing my new friend o/b the Alitalia a/c and personally secured him in his seatbelt, covered him with blankets, propped up several pillows behind his back, demonstrated all the mechanical goodies on his business class seat, and spoke to him in a universal language that he understood…compassion! I then advised the purser of his many hours of torment as he sat alone helplessly and forgotten outside of a TWA WC.. When all was said and done and it was time for me to exit, I once again knelt down in the aisle beside him, hugged him, kissed his forehead and whispered *ciao mi amico*. He squeezed my hands tightly and placed them on his heart. Once again his eyes filled with tears, as did mine. This time however, they were tears of joy rolling down his sweet little face, as he expressed immeasurable gratitude, in lieu of disparaging solitude!

DOWN THE AISLE

To properly convey the following scenario, I must preface this story by paraphrasing Sofia Petrillo's illustrious words from the hit television show, The Golden Girls...picture this...afternoon shift as gate agent at Pan Am, JFK/London flight, full 747, crowded gate area, restless passengers waiting to board.

As I made the pre-boarding announcements at the podium, sprinting towards the busy gate from across the terminal, knocking down everything in their path, were a bride and groom dressed in their complete wedding regalia yelling we're here, we're here, waaait! The bride's shrieking voice was a spine tingler and as the newlyweds approached the gate, they were huffing and puffing and almost blew us all down. Both were calorically challenged, or as they say in today's vernacular, passengers of size....she, in her floor-length poofy gown and veil and he in tux schlepping two huge carry-ons, while sweating profusely.

We all congratulated the happy couple, told them to calm down, relax and then pointed to the restrooms so they could change into comfortable traveling clothes. The blushing bride with sweat beads dripping down her cherry red face ignored our invitation to change, vehemently declaring it was their wedding day *and* night. My colleagues and I tried to discourage this lunacy since it was not only a question of discomfort for them, but also a comfort and safety issue for all the passengers and crew. My diplomatic attempts to dissuade them fell on deaf ears.

The tenacious bride took it one step further by insisting on an upgrade. I pulled up their reservation on the computer even though it was disruptive since my colleagues were busy pulling boarding passes. The "Blissfuls" had purchased a low coach fare well in advance believing that since it was their wedding day, who'd be so heartless as to not bump them up to first class! We would have considered it, however, the bride was an idiot. We advised her that it would depend on the first class load factor.

During the boarding process, and I know you can all relate, it gets a little crazy and it's a hectic time for the agents. Passengers have a tendency to ask redundant questions up at the podium, not realizing how time is of the essence. I told her we'd advise her after general boarding was completed. Five annoying minutes later, she returned to the podium using locker room profanity and insinuated that they were entitled to an upgrade. Her pecker-head husband just sat there and never uttered a word. At that point, the Ralph Cramdenesque big mouth made the decision for us…absolutely no upgrade! Needless to say, when we advised her nix, zero, nada, nothing, no way Jose, she became incensed and proceeded to scream at us saying what a bleeping airline this was …and bleep you, followed by more smutty bleeps and that she'd never fly Pan Am again. Our silenced reaction to that was…PROMISE!!!

Unbeknownst to her, I did block two extra seats for them and isolated their stupidity to the rear of the a/c. When boarding had completed, they were truly a memorable sight to behold. The infuriated little Mrs. angrily stomped up the jetway like Brunhilda with the groom in tow balancing the wedding gown train with one hand and their two carry-ons with the other. Once they had enplaned, I went o/b to advise the purser of a gate-check and of this corpulent bridezilla's behavior and she would not upgrade them either. Under any other circumstances, we would have happily acknowledged their nuptials with first class accommodations and *complimentary* champagne.

I think we can all form a visual of the disgruntled couple as they walked "down the aisle" to the rear for their seats. After the a/c pushed back from the gate, we were once again thoroughly perplexed at the less then pragmatic decision these newlyweds made. We wondered, how they would be able to sit on a six hour trans-atlantic flight in their wedding attire. Talk about chafing! And how would they indulge in their undeniably favorite pastime….eating? Another crude but true visual was that of the bodacious bride relieving herself in the teensy weensy toilets! How would she manage the proverbial wipe? Not a pretty picture!. The airborne bride squatting on the potty surely added a new dimension to the term *air-head*!

PAN AM FLIGHT 103........LOCKERBIE

December 21, 1988....a day in aviation infamy that will forever remain enmeshed in the hearts of mankind. The Christmas season for me had already been plagued with the upheaval of a seven year relationship that was meeting its demise. Weight loss, insomnia, depression and loneliness amidst the holiday festivities were my precursors to the initial stages of the mourning process. Never having experienced such emotional numbness, my daily functionality was robotic at best. Working at Pan Am's Worldport afforded me a few hours of soul-stirring relief since it entailed afternoon/evening shifts with bustling holiday travelers that kept me immersed in work.

The day began as usual with a 2:30 p. m. general briefing which consisted of Pan Am's daily flight movements along with a roster of both operational and pax information that required special attention. My usual assignment was working a gate that operated three simultaneous flights. After the briefing, my colleagues and I went to gate 24/25/26, which was already deluged with queues of anxious holiday travelers.

Approximately 4:00 p. m., while in the midst of the hectic workload, two Pan Am VIP's whom I had known, approached the gate and asked me to bring my belongings and follow them. Their mood was somber and my immediate reaction was that I'd be terminated since my pensive disposition was obviously transparent. En route to one of their private offices, not a word was spoken until we were all behind closed doors. It was then, that my personal pain transcended into grief unlike anything that I had ever experienced. I was advised that Pan Am's flight 103 had just crashed shortly after takeoff from London's Heathrow airport. Accurate details had not yet been determined other than the 747 jumbo jet touched down at Heathrow at noon (GMT) from Los Angeles and San Francisco. The aircraft was routinely cleaned, catered, fueled, and bags were off/onloaded during the standard two hour turnaround time while it was parked on the tarmac. The 747 was guarded by Pan Am's own security company by the name of Alert Security. This company proved to be disastrous since their young employees at Frankfurt airport where the first leg of the flight originated, had no formal security training. Some of them were hair dressers and store clerks.

Upon arrival at Heathrow, the Frankfurt pax's transited to the awaiting jumbo jet and boarded the a/c along with the additional pax's that were heading home for the holidays to New York's JFK airport. I was advised that a possible mechanical brought Pan Am's Clipper Maid of the Seas down over the small town of Lockerbie, Scotland setting the entire village ablaze. Since I was a *mature* agent with life experience who was born in Germany and spoke the mother tongue fluently, my assignment, along with many colleagues, was to work the cataclysmic flight 103.

The NTSB (National Transportation Safety Board) was formed in the mid 1960's and legitimatized as a federal government agency by former President Clinton. It's primary function is to coordinate guidelines and directives to federal sub agencies when aviation/transportation disasters occur. The ARC, American Red Cross, DOS, Dept. of State, DOJ, Dept. of Justice, FAA ,Federal Aviation Administration and the FBI are just a few agencies that are under the NTSB umbrella. They conversely disseminate information statewide and locally and implement a course of action in support of the airline per se and its disaster victims and families. A local base of operation must be created consisting of state and local emergency response and crisis teams. The airline is responsible to notify next of kin, provide lodging, transportation, meals, clergy, medical doctors, emotional and logistic support at the crash site and at points of departure and arrival, in this case, JFK airport. The Dept. of State is responsible for coordinating interaction with the Foreign Embassies when disasters occur outside of the U.S.

Sequentially, official airline "disaster mode" tasks were relegated to Pan Am execs and staff and the course of action began. Since 103 was due that evening, securing privacy for the family members and protecting them from the media was paramount. On the arrival boards, in lieu of the standard ETA for PA 103, the signage read, *See agents at Area C & D. Certain* agents were posted there and had the task of escorting families to the First Class Lounge. Together they walked silently through the terminals to avoid subjecting them to public scrutiny. The agents were not permitted to disclose any details and were advised only to say that information was forthcoming once they arrived at the Lounge, which by then, had been roped off and designated a High Security Area. It was transformed along with other JFK offices, into an Emergency Operations Center to facilitate the necessary services.

Within the hour, local hotels purveyed catering by setting up tables around the perimeter of the lounge supplying nonstop food and alcohol. Phones with toll free numbers were placed on tables throughout the lounge enabling families to make calls worldwide.

Everyone that was assigned 103 assembled in the lounge and was relegated a specific assignment. Myself and other colleagues were designated *contact* people. As area C & D agents escorted families into the lounge one at a time, I immediately had to verify the victim's identity via the flight manifest that we each had on a clipboard which listed the names of the 270 pax's and crew o/b flight 103. When I asked the family to disclose the name of the pax they were meeting, I was required to secure vital information such as their relationship to the victim and contact numbers. Maintaining a modem of decorum was a priority. Not having been professionally or psychologically trained in working disasters of such magnitude, inner strength and numbness enabled me to carry out my duties without falling apart emotionally as I stoically confirmed their worst nightmare….as per Pan Am….Fl. 103 had *crashed.*

All the families that I personally received at the door, were my responsibility for the duration of the disaster. Because it was not immediately deemed as an act of terrorism, details provided to us by management trickled in and were sketchy at best. The priority at that point was for Pan Am to reconcile the flight manifest via 103's boarding passes that were lifted at the departure gate at Heathrow, along with the check-in list and the final gate check. An error in disseminating the manifest would have been as devastating as the crash itself. It was also imperative that any information we acquired had to be confirmed and disclosed as it came in that night from Lockerbie via London and Washington.

Pan Am's annual Christmas party was being hosted that night at one of the local hotels. In that industry, socializing at times began after 11: 00 p. m. due to airline and staff scheduling. Unaware of the crisis that awaited the world, I welcomed the opportunity to temporarily allow my heart to digress from the emotional grief I was experiencing in my personal life. Lara, my daughter and wonderful traveling companion, who was fifteen at that time was my date for the party. She had been en route to the airport from Long Island via a car service and had no knowledge of her impending anguish. We confirmed everything the night before since she had been staying with her father during Christmas vacation. The car would drop her off at the terminal and she was to meet me at my usual departure gate at 6:00 p. m. to hang out and "people" watch as she had in the past while waiting for me. Our plan was to first have dinner after my shift, then partake in the girly-girl ritual of party prepping. In the blink of an eye, this monumental tragedy changed everything. From one of the managers offices, I called her father's house to divert the car from coming to JFK and instead to go straight to our apartment in Forest Hills, but she had already left and cell phones back then were non existent.

Approximately 5:30, the relentless and despicable pursuit for media sensationalism already began at the terminal. Hundreds of reporters swarmed in like vultures ready to attack innocent prey. They tried to force their way beyond the sealed-off ropes to gain access into the first class lounge. They pushed through barricades that protected the escorted families during their terrifying walk from "Area C and D" towards the lounge where catastrophic realities awaited them.

Since clearance had already been arranged for my daughter, my colleagues at the gate called me when she arrived and one of the agents escorted her down. Twenty minutes later, most upset, she called me from a phone booth just outside the roped off area. Not having any details, as she approached the lounge, the media bombarded her with questions thinking that she came to meet a pax from 103. Her only refuge was to secure herself in the booth adjacent to the lounge until I came and got her. In doing so, I waded through the mass of insensitivity and insolence, pushed the cameras and microphones out of our faces and together we fought our way back to the lounge.

The emotional journey that befell Lara, myself and my colleagues was unsparing. The emotional journey that befell the *victim's* families was horrifying. Ten feet from the lounge doors, we witnessed an agent escorting a woman who had been traumatized two weeks prior by the sudden death of one child. Her other child was o/b 103! The reporters attempted to "get the scoop" by prematurely asking her what she knew about the crash. The curdling scream and the thud as she hit the floor remains infused in our hearts today, as clear as the moment it happened. Spotlighted and lying unconscious on the floor, the cameras kept rolling..... the reporters kept probing. Her torment was front page news worldwide. Even after the woman collapsed, the nefarious reporters continued questioning her.

Once back inside, I quickly briefed Lara and positioned her at a corner table and then returned to my post at the front door while intermittently checking on her. The ambiance in that room had increasingly escalated to a daunting surrealism. Watching in disbelief, Lara knew she needed to help in whatever capacity she could.... offering her shoulders to cry on, her hands to hold and her heart to those destroyed. A father whose son was o/b came through the doors very angrily and immediately said to me, this better be a *serious* mechanical to cause such an outrageous delay. How I wished that were the case. I humbly asked him for the name of the pax that he and his wife were picking up. He lunged forward and pulled my uniform jacket towards him, screaming in pain... don't you dare tell me my son is dead...don't you *dare!* Under the circumstances, as an emissary for Pan Am's horrific tragedy, how could I have expected anyone to react rationally! While fighting back my own flood of tears, I calmly advised him of the crash. His wife tried to maintain her composure long enough to ask if there were survivors and I told her, it had not yet been determined. Despite the devastating news, the families desperately clung onto the hope that somehow, somewhere, their loved ones were still alive. Chaplains and doctors were readily at hand to console or medicate. Many people went into shock while others simply fainted in my arms. Many fell to their knees and wept uncontrollably as I cradled them like babies.

The local Pan Am VIP's started converging in the lounge in an attempt to disseminate details to us from Lockerbie. We were advised that at 8:00 p. m. the CEO would come in and hold a private conference to update the families which would be followed by a national press conference outside of the doors. When Tom P. entered the lounge and stood on a make shift podium, the collective sounds of everyone's heartbeat was deafening. All terrified eyes in that room faced him, and all arms were tightly interlocked with one another as they braced themselves for the unimaginable. And then emotionally, he made the official announcement..... there were no survivors. For the second time that night, emotional paralysis befell the families and their unbearable pain could be heard around the world. We all held on to them, for had we let go, they would have fallen to the ground. Hours prior to the crash, my personal pain pierced my heart with every breathe I took. However, the agony around me that evening engendered a soulful epiphany and a self-analytical reality check, i.e., the *true* love of my life was standing right next to me! She was alive and well. I could touch her, see her, hold her. It was then that my pain took on a new dimension. I cried *with* Lara that night, not *for* her, unlike all those traumatized people in that room who had brutally just lost *their* Laras. The slightest glimmer of hope for survival had been shattered and our tasks were re-assigned from rescue mode to recovery mode. We stayed with our families indefinitely that night and Pan Am made arrangements for them to fly to Lockerbie the next morning. To this day, the most amazing show of strength that Lara and I had ever witnessed, was that of a loving African American family who was among my group from the onset. To help console them and the other amazing people, I shared my personal secular beliefs that a higher power of whatever name one wishes to use, had a greater agenda for these beloved victims and that our destined paths in life have unrelenting hurdles.

The woman who lost her husband asked us all to sit in a circle and hold hands as she led us in prayer. This amazing family comforted everyone despite their own torment. Their impenetrable faith gave them the courage to accept the reality bestowed upon them that night. Lara and I were so moved by these incredible people, we just stood there and sobbed as they reached out with genuine love to everyone in that room.

I was asked by one of the VP's to fly to Lockerbie on the 6: a. m. charter with my families. My decision was instantaneous. I respectfully declined. As much as I bonded with everyone, my need to be with my child was overwhelming and she too needed me, for we shared a historical disaster that cut deep into our own reservoir of raw emotions. Around midnight, our families were escorted to JFK hotels. My thoughts were, how do we say goodbye. Would we have the courage to tell them to be strong, knowing full well that their journey to hell would intensify within a few hours and persist for the rest of their lives?

After unending paperwork, everyone who worked that room desperately needed to be with one another to try and comprehend the events that had taken place. We wondered about the poor souls and families who were wrapping Christmas presents in their quaint homes in Lockerbie earlier that evening. Life was simple for this sleepy little village, until the night the plane fell out of the sky! 1988 had its share of clandestine tragedies in the US and in other countries that were deemed acts of terrorism. While working the "room" that night, myself and several of my colleagues had been informed by upper management that 103 was presumably brought down by a bomb. It was also established that night that Pan Am officials and Washington D.C. were aware of this time-framed bomb threat, since American Embassies were put on alert several weeks prior to Dec. 21st.

As the investigative events unfolded from month to month and year to year, even to this day, the truth remains illusive. It is the epitome of insult and disrespect to the victims o/b Fl. 103 who were violently murdered, to their families, to the families in Lockerbie and to all who were and still are involved in the investigations. Those innocent passengers did not know that they had only 38 minutes of life remaining once Clipper Maid Of The Seas lifted off the runway at Heathrow and headed North toward Scotland. So too, we remain clueless with justifiable indignation because the bureaucratic secrecy of 103 has been shrouded at the expense of *all* the above and at the expense of our own security here in the U.S.

Dec. 21, 1988 was the day the lounge was transformed from an opulent inner sanctum for the privileged first class passenger, to an urbane chamber of horrors for the next of kin.

DILDO DILEMMA

The average flight day's success was usually determined by an on-time arrival and departure. Staff went to great lengths to turn the a/cs around in their allotted ground time which is regulated by ATC. They do not just hang out at a gate indefinitely. They have designated "slot" times and are pushed back to hardstands if the slot time is exceeded.... a no-win situation for everyone involved.

Unbeknownst to the public, a/c's in general, are continuously airborne. Once they arrive at a gate and the engines are shut off, the clock starts ticking. There is only a short window of ground time in which staff must off/onload pax's, baggage and cargo, get mechanically checked, catered, cleaned, and fueled. The standard turnaround time for international flights is two hours. As a result, any delays in landing or departures cause a domino effect worldwide. Each flight had its physical and mental challenges necessitating endurance and hours of extensive paperwork.

One summer evening, everything was moving along at its usual intensified pace. With only ten minutes to spare before the 5:00 p. m. ETD, all 408 pax's were o/b safely buckled in their seatbelts waiting for the departure. While our handling agents were securing the cargo doors, and as I made my usual last run into the cockpit for the final briefing, one of our baggage handlers raced up into the cockpit to advise us that they started offloading a bag from the cargo hold. They heard a buzzing noise coming from a suitcase just three tense minutes before pushback. An apparent delay became inevitable as our primary concerns of course, were safety and security.

The captain and I went down to the tarmac and we waited rampside (aircraft parking) for Port Authority police while the buzzing bag was offloaded. Once it was retrieved, I sprinted back up the stairs into the cabin and made an announcement asking that the person whose bagtag number matched the one just offloaded needed to identify themselves and accompany me down to the tarmac. Everyone started looking around to see who the culprit was that held up their departure. After a minute or so, all eyes were on this elegantly dressed middle-aged woman. She calmly stood up never making eye contact and followed me down the stairs.

Security procedures mandated that the woman open her bag in front of port authority police. All the onboard pax's that had starboard (right side) window seats, were in full view of this tarmac tryst. She was most defiant and refused to cooperate. Finally, after advising her of the legal ramifications and the prospect of not allowing her back on the a/c, she opened her suitcase. Low and behold, fully encased in a black velvet bag, tassels and all, (quite nice actually), was a super-sized vibrator humming along at some serious RPM's! Holding up the a/c because of a harebrained dildo debacle had its repercussions. Our collective thoughts were to take her tactless ten-incher and ream her an additional orifice, but that would have been unprofessional. In lieu of an apology from this horny halfwit, we all felt that her humiliation level was abundantly sufficient, especially when she was told to remove the batteries in "plane" sight of everyone. From sheer embarrassment, I'm sure she would have preferred to fly in the cargo hold rather than walk back up into the a/c and be deemed as the in-flight slut.

The distressed damsel's dildo dilemma had to be a life altering experience for her and an exasperating one for me because of the unnecessary involvement of PA police and the waste of everyone's time.

Subsequently, her bag was put back in the cargo hold, the doors were shut, the captain gave us the thumbs up, the chocks were removed from the wheels and off she went.

We took a useless 17 minute delay. When I went back to my office, I had to think of the appropriate terminology for the mandatory "Incident Report" for Germany explaining the delay. It was tricky! Would "Distressed Dildo Delay" be politically correct? I laughed and thought, what a dumb idiot! Was bringing it to Germany imperative, batteries and all or was she anticipating a dildo *emergency* upon landing?

POCKET MONEY

I've often felt that intellect and intelligence are sometimes misconstrued for wisdom and common sense. One would think a successful doctor knows that when traveling abroad a passport is mandatory.

I had been called to the check-in area by an agent who advised me that Dr. and Mrs. Whatever were checking in and the twit left his passport at home. He had argued with the agent and vehemently insisted that his New York State driver's license would suffice as proof of U.S. citizenship. The agent politely explained that she couldn't issue him a boarding pass without a passport and specifically pointed to the required documentation that was printed on his ticket. His immediate thought process was to intimidate her into submission by publicly discrediting her competence. When the seasoned agent wasn't phased by his egregious tantrums, he insisted on speaking with a supervisor.

Knowing the problem before approaching the fool, I thought perhaps reversed psychology would rectify this situation. I introduced myself and gave him the courtesy of speaking first. After his stupid soliloquy, I smiled and said...Dr. Whatever, surely an intelligent and worldly traveler such as yourself knows that a passport is mandatory for travel outside the U.S. In reality I wanted to say, YOU DUMB SCHMUCK! The word that I quietly mouthed *rhymed* with schmuck! This duplicitous jerk would not accept my dose of reality and demanded on speaking with a man, thinking he could bully me into rescinding my decision. I calmly called Adrian on his radio to come to the check-in counter since the good doctor wanted to speak to someone with male genitalia. I left mine home that day!

Adrian and I were very much in tune with one another and he knew precisely how to intervene. As he approached, I excused myself and Adrian took over. The doctor told him we refused to issue his rightful boarding pass. He took his anger up a notch when Adrian validated the mandatory passport requirement. Adrian then asked if he would like to speak with the Station Manager. The Dr. exclaimed *YES*, finally, someone with authority! After making him wait twenty minutes, guess who reappeared? Realizing he was defeated, he took me by my elbow, led me a few feet away from his wife, opened his wallet and discreetly folded a $500 bill into the palm of my hand. My reaction was....what an insult. First of all, how dare you touch me and secondly, what a parsimonious bribe! I regaled with delight in telling him that no amount of money will get him on the a/c. This dickweed then said to me "name your price, within reason of course. "Even though valuable time was being wasted, his arrogance was exasperating, so it was time to get out the big guns.

Laughing inwardly, I told him to walk over to IAT, look for the Immigration officer with a big gold shiny badge, tell him you're a "healer" wink wink…a private JFK code I slyly mumbled, and if he gives you clearance to fly without a passport, come on back and you're good to go! It was tough keeping a straight face while I watched him drool with delight. His wife stayed with their luggage while he went off on a fool's errand. Ten minutes later, he returned and I thought to myself, this should be good. The good doctor advised me that the officer said *no problem* and that all he had to do was have someone fedex the passport to an address in Germany for re-entry into USA. Now, surreptitiously, could that have been arranged? That's another story! I had enough of his crap, called his bluff, and insisted that we both walk back over to IAT to the officer who authorized his travel. Magically, his acrimonious demeanor changed when he realized his blatant lie didn't fly….and neither did he!

I advised him that while he went for his *pretend* approval to IAT, I canceled his reservations with the airline and that he would not be accepted on any of our future flights. His wife was clearly embarrassed by his infantile behavior. After humbly apologizing to me, she glared at him with contempt while mumbling a litany of shocking obscenities. That was cool! Needless to say, there were no smoochy farewells as she walked away and proceeded up to the departure gate alone, leaving Pinochio behind. As he stood there like a total jackass and speechless in disbelief of what had transpired, it was my turn to take *him* by the elbow, as he did earlier to mine, and escort him to the door. I took such sadistic pleasure in telling the fool that his pocket money nor his title overrode common sense or the law, and to……..have a *great* day!

NEVER.........NEVERLAND

When I beneath the cold red earth am sleeping and life
has closed its door, will there be for me any eye weeping,
that I am no more......anonymous

(SOP) standard operating procedure for our inbound flights
from Germany entailed my meeting the a/c upon arrival at
JFK and going o/b before the pax's deplaned. The purser
(chief flight attendant) and the captain would brief me of
any incidents that might have occurred in-flight. As unique
as some situations were, crews were always well trained in
handling airborne nuances.

On this particular Sunday afternoon when the a/c arrived
at the gate, as soon as the captain turned off the engines,
the purser immediately opened the forward cabin door.
She was ashen in color and the expression on her face was
ghastly as if she were ready to regurgitate previous meals. As
an experienced and seasoned crew member for many years,
she had a charming disposition and always calmly handled
unexpected surprises. Her first words to me as I boarded the
a/c were, Oh My God, Oh My God, this was eight hours of

hell. While walking towards her, a repugnant odor hit me like a ton of bricks, as though everyone's barf bag was filled to the max. My unsolicited reaction was HOLY SHIT, to which she emphatically responded with PRECISELY, as she handed me an in-flight Incident Report. She along with the other crew members, verbally gave me their individual accounts of the events that had transpired.

Two hours into the flight, a pax was heard crying from the rear of the cabin. As one of the f/a's (flight attendant's) walked towards the commotion, she was overwhelmed by a terrible odor that emanated from the back. A female pax had urinated and defecated in her seat and subsequently continued doing so throughout the flight. The pax's that were sitting near her were physically repulsed and in a timely fashion, one by one began vomiting due to the intolerable stench that permeated the area. Opening windows was not an option.

The crew sprayed special deodorizers posthaste that temporarily masked the offensive air which circulated throughout the fuselage.

The load factor on that trans-Atlantic flight was 360 pax's in lieu of the usual 408. Having 48 empty seats, the f/a's scrambled to relocate everyone that sat in the rear. They closed off a section by blocking as many rows as possible, along with one of the bathrooms to keep her isolated. While that was being done, two of the f/a's discreetly tried to take her into the toilet to remove her soiled clothing, wash her up and dress her in clean clothes that they voluntarily took out of their own personal carryon luggage. According to the purser, when they gently tried to lift her out of the seat, she began sobbing like a little child clenching on for dear life to her mother's arms in fear of being hurt or taken away. Unable to move her, the crew placed blankets around her lap and on the floor to absorb the urine and to keep it from flowing under nearby seats or down the aisles when the a/c banked. They all displayed extraordinary compassion and went far beyond the call of duty.

After observing her for awhile, the purser determined that the pax was incoherent and had no comprehension of her surroundings, nor did she seem capable of speaking any languages per se. Pitiful tears just flowed from her hollow eyes as she grunted while tightly clutching her armrests. At first, given the extenuating circumstances, the captain decided to turn around and head back to Germany, even though they had been airborne for two hours over the Atlantic. After a briefing with the crew, they agreed to proceed to JFK since the woman was not disruptive nor were the other pax's in any imminent danger.

Under normal circumstances, each f/a is assigned to work a section of the a/c. The crew took it upon themselves to take turns in working the rear where she sat pathetically alone in her own feces and body fluids while perpetually rocking back and forth. As grueling as it was, the crew had to constantly placate the other pax's since they were literally sickened by the situation at hand. Despite the putrid stench, two in-flight meals and beverage services still had to be conducted in as congenial manner as possible. They had to scour, serve and smile.

One of the f/a's anxiously told the story of how her swimming prowess enabled her to hold her breath long enough to speedily throw the soiled blankets that were wrapped around the woman in a plastic bag, replace them with clean ones and place a pre-cut hot lunch on the woman's tray table. When all was done, she raced into one of the bathrooms, gasped for air and feverishly scrubbed her hands. After the pathetic soul devoured her lunch, another f/a went back to the off limits section and removed her lunch tray. The f/a wiped her dirty hands and face with a hot towel, and for the first time, eye contact was made. They exchanged a warm smile as though she finally understood no one was going to hurt her, at least not at 35,000 ft. high. Having gained a level of trust, the f/a took it a step further. She retrieved the woman's bag from the overhead bin, looked for her passport and pro-actively filled out the mandatory immigration forms that are given to pax's in-flight prior to landing. They are required for entry by Immigration and Customs.

Upon the a/c's final approach into JFK, and despite the horrendous ordeal the majority of the pax's had to endure for so many hours, the crew was astonished by everyone's overall compassion. Some pax's were of course incensed that the airline would allow such a "disturbed" individual on the flight and understandably so. They realized nothing could've been done and the crew was commended for their outstanding professionalism even though barf bags became facial attachments for several of the pax's throughout the encapsulated airborne ordeal.

We all know how it gets after sitting on an a/c during long-range flights. Upon landing, it's a dash towards the exit doors to get off as expeditiously as possible. After standing in the forward cabin for only a few minutes for the briefing, I couldn't fathom being trapped like that without any form of relief for over eight hours. Most of the pax's remained civil while deplaning and in typical German fashion, they waited their turn to exit the aisles, however, it was indeed a regimented race to get out. The f/a whom she trusted stood in the aft cabin near the rear galley. Verbally and via hand gestures she told the reticent woman to remain in her seat, which is the SOP for handicapped pax's. I called for a wheelchair knowing she would be escorted straight through to the arrivals terminal. With only a few pax's left to deplane, the crew and I braced ourselves for the abhorrent task of bringing her from the rear cabin to the front and into the wheelchair without any further episodes. However, despite the smell and appearance, somehow, the woman covertly walked off and followed the crowd to Immigration. Her documentation was obviously in order, otherwise I would've been called by an INS officer. We assumed that given the nature of the woman's mental limitations, she'd be met at the airport by family and then....case closed! After I deplaned to continue my duties, I wondered what emotions had been stirred up in everyone and questioned my personal reaction, had I been subjected to such a horrific situation. Eventually, I thought the *crazy lady* would just be a topic of conversation and the mundane lives of all the pax's o/b that flight would recommence.

During turnarounds, there were many reasons which generated potential delays and that surely was one. Her seat had to be replaced and the cabin required fumigation. The a/c could not leave the gate until it was deemed completely airworthy. Fortunately, Delta, our contracted ground maintenance handler, successfully installed a new seat within the allotted time while Triangle Aviation Services cleaned up to the best of their ability. The remainder of the afternoon's outbound operations went smoothly. For all intended purposes, I was home free when those melodious words, off the blocks, were announced from the tarmac, i.e. actual time of departure when wooden blocks under aircraft wheels are removed.

In situations where a/c's take a delay on the taxiway en route to or from the runway due to congestion or inclement weather, it is not the responsibility of the airline's ground staff per se. This unpalatable situation was atypical and thanks to our vendors, they were successfully able to avert a departure delay at the gate in spite of the internal condition of the aft cabin.

After the departure, I thought all went operationally well in Claudia's world that day. I contently meandered back to the office and began the tedious afterflight work. The high heels immediately came off my aching feet from all the running around. To unwind before beginning, I went down the hall barefoot to the KLM lounge for a glass of wine, good Dutch cheese, a few laughs and the daily gossip with staff. Feeling all warm and fuzzy in my skippy-day mood, I returned to the office and settled in with pen in hand. At 7:00 p. m., my happy hour came to an abrupt and evil end.

We received a call from Customs that an LTU pax had been wandering around aimlessly and since she was technically still the airline's responsibility, someone needed to come and get her. My complacency instantly turned into adversity. It was apparent that no one came to the airport to meet this pathetic soul.

Where the in-flight crew's responsibility ended, mine had just begun and going home at a reasonable hour became a figment of my imagination. My assistant offered to walk over to IAT to get her. He called from his radio on the way back and told me to brace myself for a unique challenge. He brought the pax to the departure terminal which by then was empty, in lieu of bringing her to our office. He told me to take deep breaths and to wrap my uniform scarf around my mouth and nose just before I approached her. I was aghast and absolutely *shocked* when I saw this fragile, 34-yr old woman. She had porcelain skin, short brown pixie hair, wearing an old tee shirt with denim overalls and flip-flops on her filthy little feet. The stench that emanated from her was overwhelming. She was meek, sweet-tempered and had a benevolent warm smile.

I asked her questions in German, but soon realized she was mentally inept and could not speak. Her only sounds were grunts and cries as she vacillated between both. Adrian was told by the Custom agent that she had no luggage other than a small kiddie backpack that I gingerly removed from her shoulders. It contained an old plastic wallet with the equivalent of only ten dollars in Romanian money, one hooded sweatshirt, one tee shirt, a small comb, a brand new Romanian passport, used for the first time for passage from Bucharest via Germany to JFK, but no return ticket back home! In that dirty old velcro wallet was the clue to her well-planned disposal....a newspaper clipping from 1971 about the opening of Disneyworld in Orlando. It was barely legible and yellowed because of its actual print age some twenty plus years prior. It actually fell apart in my hands as I tried to read it. Her hollow brown eyes lit up like a child's on Christmas morning. She grinned uncontrollably from ear to ear. Both Adrian and I were emotionally sickened and fought back our tears. Bursting with joy, she uttered the words Florida, Florida, Disney, Disney. It was then that we understood why she was standing in front of us. This poor woman had been forsaken by her caretakers and deserted under the guise of visiting Disneyworld.

It was incomprehensible to us that fellow human beings were capable of discarding life as they would an old shoe, or when functionality simply ceased. Had society become so jaded with the myriad of murders, wars, racism, and apathy, that turning the other cheek became the better part of valor? I refused to believe that people could do something so diabolical, yet, there she stood, with such sweet innocence, as she pointed to the faded article with infantile exhilaration. It just broke our hearts because we knew her dream would never become a reality. Adrian had located a Romanian speaking agent, hoping the woman would respond in her native language, but she didn't. He stayed with her while I went back to the office to carefully read the purser's inflight incident report again.

I called our Ops (operations) in Germany which is manned 24/7. They checked her reservations in the computer and found a comment in her booking, which stated that the pax required onboard assistance to restrooms due to a slight mental disability. Written comments are made by a reservation/check-in agent if there are any specific requests or discrepancies noted during the check-in process. Ops contacted the agent at the airport who checked her in earlier that morning for the West bound flight to JFK. The initials of the agent were in the pax's computerized transaction. This is SOP with every airline, should there be any repercussions….case in point. Ops was able to ascertain the details as to how this all manifested. Because of the seriousness and the legalities involved, an immediate investigation began. The Ops agent and I communicated back and forth all night to determine just where and when the system's *and* the pax breakdown began.

I had a far more exacerbating dilemma…what to do with her? My first priority was to scrounge up some clean clothes because the smell of several loads of dried poop and urine made us all gag. I went to the lost & found office and they offered to look for any unclaimed clothing that was available. I then called the Port Authority police and hoped that friends I knew were on duty. That not being the case on a late Sunday night, I presented my plight anyway and their only suggestion was that they would fill out proverbial reports and bring her to the local hospital for psychological evaluation. I felt she didn't stand a chance in hell of surviving and graciously declined. Just then, one of the KLM handling agents came into my office with a pair of grossly neglected pajama pants and a mangy tee shirt that she found in an old unclaimed suitcase. I was so ecstatic and planted a huge kiss on her forehead. Adrian managed to keep her perched on the bench by giving firm yet non-threatening directives tantamount to a dog's commands, e.g. sit, stay.

He did some of my reports for me that night while I figured out what to do next. At 9:00 p. m. I sent him home since there wasn't much else he could do. Then, another disgusting task awaited me since. Her appearance and odor was unbearable. I took her to the ladies room and handed her the tattered pants and shirt. After gentle coaxing, she timidly removed her soiled overalls. I pointed to the garbage can and then to her underwear that was infused to her skin. Reluctantly, she took them off. I attempted to clean her hands and face, but she started crying and backed away. I mimicked washing and she slowly came over and put her hands in the sink, never taking her eyes off of me. In my estimation, she had been a feral child. My thoughts ran amok as I mentally recapped my contractual LTU employment agreement. Coercing a mentally ill woman to disrobe in an airport bathroom was not in my job description. It was all *so* debasing. Enrage and self-pity had taken over, yet I repeatedly kept telling myself she's a human being, don't throw her away along with the feces infested clothes and treat her with kindness.

After regaining composure, I handed her paper towels. My compassion must have momentarily registered in her disconnected world because with a tender smile, she reached out to touch my hand and while awkwardly drying herself off, she displayed a level of trust.

After the bathroom breakthrough, I took her hand and we walked upstairs to Pizza Hut which was in the process of closing. Fortunately, the guys knew me and reheated two incredibly stale pizzas. She was ravenous and ate like an animal and as expected, totally devoid of any table etiquette. Her only sounds were grunts. We then walked over to IAT to speak with the Traveler's Aid Society to see if they would provide shelter for one night while I secured passage back to Romania on a flight the next morning. The rep saw that I was in *dire* need of their services. She advised me that she could only provide one way bus fare to NYC to go to the consulate and one meal voucher at a JFK eatery. She displayed apathy, no empathy! That was the extent of her "aid". For a job such as that, compassion is a prerequisite. She seemed to have been inconvenienced by my desperate attempts for help. Her isolated attitude was not the norm, since Traveler's Aid Society had always been a blessing for stranded people. As exhausted and angry as I was with a zero batting average, I refused to acquiesce. We walked all the way back to the departure hall where I once again perched her on "the bench". Despite my mounting frustrations, discarding this poor creature was not an option. I had the luxury of going home…, eventually. I was loved, I was rational, nor was I ever abandoned. After all, she was a human being. We were kindred sisters.

Feeling defeated and up against brick walls, I called acquaintances who managed a JFK hotel and advised them of my downhill plight. They immediately offered assistance and said they would meet us in the lobby. It was 11:00 p. m. when we arrived at the hotel via autolink, Like happy little people, we all got into the elevator and proceeded to the room the managers set aside for her. I turned down the bed and once again took her into the bathroom, and mimicked washing. We all made sure she saw the security guard who was placed outside of her door until the morning. Before leaving the room, I pointed to the clock and held up seven fingers, hoping she felt reassured that I'd be back to get her. She grunted and grinned, we smiled and left.

Any costs incurred for unforeseen services such as hotels, meals, transport etc., are generally paid for by the carrier based on the airline manager's discretion. The hotel managers also made arrangements to have breakfast sent to the room at 8 a. m. on Monday morning at which time I was going to pick her. After many grueling hours of drama, on the way back from the hotel to my office, I breathed a sigh of relief that she was safe, at least for that night. Our airline did not operate Monday flights from JFK at that time so I called a manager friend at Lufthansa and explained the circumstances to her. Without hesitation, she made the necessary arrangements for a flight the next day and buffered the aft cabin.

Airlines in general have an unwritten code of reciprocity with one another. More often than not, they're most helpful in re-accommodating pax's. Lufthansa's assistance was exemplary of this implicit mutuality. Airports become your second home and the employees become family. When a crisis occurs, they rally together and become a part of the solution.

Foolishly assuming that she was sound asleep under supervision, l finally headed home at 1:00 a. m.

In order of priority, I took off my uniform, threw it in the outside garbage bin, took a hot shower and wrapped my pruny body in a pair of flannels.

I was starving and too lazy to make anything to eat, so a box of Chips Ahoy cookies and a quart of milk hit the spot.

Shortly after a few minutes of channel surfing to unwind, I exploded into sleep only to be viciously awakened at 3:00 a. m. by a call from the hotel manager frantically advising me that their guest was gone! Somehow she walked out of her room unnoticed. Prior to calling me, a search of the entire hotel and the outside grounds had already been made. According to the "INSECURITY" guard who was assigned the simple task of securing the room, he had repeatedly knocked on the door at approximately 2:30 a. m. When there was no answer, he had the front desk call her room and they notified the managers who lived on site. Realizing he obviously left his post or that he slept on the job wasn't exactly rocket science. There wasn't anything deviant about her, therefore, I was certain that she did not maliciously sneak out. When the managers opened the room, the bed had not even been slept in, nor were any of the bathroom amenities used. I was just devastated that in the middle of the night, in a questionable neighborhood, this damaged child walked into oblivion.

Physically and emotionally, I was on overload and told myself that from a humanitarian perspective, I did everything possible, short of having her committed, which for me was not a feasible option and yet in my heart I was responsible for her disappearance. I castigated myself with the proverbial should haves. I called the PA police again and they put out an alert hoping she'd be found roaming the streets. We called the local precincts and hospitals, but it was an exercise in futility.

In the interim, Ops in Germany had contacted the check-in agent and the crew of that particular flight. The following was determined: The agent clearly remembered that the pax was accompanied by another woman of similar age. When the two were on the queue, they approached the counter with proper documents. The older woman did all the talking while the younger one just quietly stood there. She requested a seat in the aft cabin, stating that her sister was a bit slow and required privacy and occasional bathroom assistance. Since the agent did not feel there was anything inappropriate, she accommodated the request. However, she made a wise decision before issuing the boarding pass. She excused herself for a moment, and went into the Ops office directly behind her which was visible from the counter. There, she approached the captain who was to operate that flight and was in the process of his pre-flight briefing. She asked him to go look at the pax and assess her ability to fly since the agent felt a bit skeptical about her appearance. The captain peered from the Ops office as the agent pointed her out. He observed her from afar and felt she was not a danger to the other pax's. They both agreed that a comment in her record was necessary. She was then issued a boarding pass and both woman proceeded to the gate. Prior to 9/11, pax's were allowed to be accompanied by family etc. Since no dialogue was necessary for boarding, the older woman asked the gate agents if she could escort her sister to the a/c door and was given permission to do so. She was then taken to her seat by one of the f/a's. Just before the a/c doors closed, the crew was given the usual loadsheet, a printout of the weight and balance and information pertinent to the flight, inclusive of this pax's check-in comment entered by the agent. That was the beginning of her end!

Based on the investigation, it was determined that a woman purchased a ticket for the pax with cash at a travel agency in Bucharest, two days prior to the flight and paid full fare. That in itself was out of the norm and should have raised a red flag. According to the travel agent, the anonymous purchaser seemed nervous and in a hurry to complete the transaction. She gave a fictitious name, address and phone number as the contact and claimed the pax was her sister. The travel agent also disclosed that a roundtrip ticket was indeed purchased, but she was, as expected, a no-show.

It was and shall always remain incomprehensible to me that a human being could be rejected in such a cruel manner because she was obviously a burden to her caretakers. Her wretched existence was blatantly expendable. No one knows what happened to her in the streets of New York. It haunted me for years. One of my silly coping mechanisms has always been to neatly compartmentalize issues in my brain and deal with them in order of priority. It alleviates the all too familiar emotional overload. I tried to convince myself, that she was "somewhere safe".

When my imaginary supposition lost internal credibility, to console myself, I remembered the words of Socrates just as he was about to poison himself with hemlock…."To Die and Be Released". He couldn't bare the injustice of society that condemned him to life imprisonment. She too was unjustly imprisoned in a psychological hell. I had to believe that her possible demise was the lesser of all evils and that metaphysically, she crossed over and went home to a kinder existence. Despite *my* personal in-depth involvement, the airline's, the NYC, German and Romanian Police Departments, she was never found!

Henry Thoreau succinctly once wrote of an Indian woman who was vilified by society "No one heard the beat of her drum. No one else heard her drumbeat that thumped in the farthest reaches of her awareness." I could only have hoped that she was not cognizant of her personal depravity, that she suffered in comfort while fulfilling her flight of fancy and that she ultimately and painlessly reached her own beloved Disneyworld!

UM- PLANNED PARENTHOOD

When children travel alone between the ages of 7 and 14, they are considered UM's, (unaccompanied minors). Since they are the airline's responsibility, the ground and in-flight crews follow strict guidelines in handling these young passengers. During check-in at the departure terminal, a family member or guardian must fill out mandatory forms which contain pertinent information for the child's safety and security. These signed forms along with their travel documents are put in a plastic pouch issued by the agent and placed around the child's neck.

The adult then escorts the UM to the departure gate and when boarding commences, an agent brings the child o/b to a set of rows designated for UM's and secures the child in his pre-assigned seat. The f/a's provide in-flight goodies to keep the child occupied. Upon arrival at their final destination, the UM remains seated until the other pax's deplane. They are then taken off the a/c by an agent who brings them to Immigration, Customs and baggage claim. When all is done, the child is handed over in the arrivals terminal to a family member who must sign for his release. In general, it is an amiable, secure modus operandi and children usually consider it a fun experience.

Upon one of the arrivals, an agent called my office to advise they had a 12-year old UM, his luggage and no parents to sign for him. I asked the agent to wait half hour or so, assuming the parents encountered traffic since they were coming from Stanford, Connecticut. An hour later, still no parents. The agent brought him over to me, and in addition to my usual operational responsibilities, babysitting was added to the evening's to-do list. He was a little cutie, not at all stressed and took it in stride. After a few minutes of making small-talk, I called the UM's home. An answering machine picked up. I left a message saying they needn't be frantic with worry because their son was secure in my office. The two of us kept looking at the door and we reassured one another that any minute the distraught parents would magically appear, grab the little boy in their arms, kiss him and hug him and squeeze him all over! An hour later, it was evident that this Kodak moment was not going to happen all that soon.

Since I had to be rampside for our outbound flight, I told the UM not to move out of the office until I returned and that he was welcomed to answer my phone and take messages. Since the most hectic time for all of us was in the late afternoon, calls for me came through via Ops and our radios. Any calls received at my desk were only personal ones and it made him feel important that I relegated this responsibility to him. Being crazy busy around 4:00 p. m., the poor little guy was still patiently sitting at my desk, so I took him into operations when the outbound cockpit crew arrived from NYC to do their pre-flight briefing. He was fascinated and asked the captain to sign his log book. I thought to myself, he is just an incredibly mature young man or he's been there, done that before! I wasn't quite sure yet.

After the departure, I was certain that by the time I returned back from the tarmac, June and Ward Cleaver and the Beave would be merrily on their way back to Connecticut singing Cumbaya. Not so! He was doodling on a piece of paper at my desk and when I walked in, he anxiously looked up at me and asked if his parents had arrived. I checked with the staff again and as expected, they hadn't, which meant another long night of surprises at JFK. Since food is the way to young man's stomach, up we went to good old Pizza Hut. I put paperwork aside for awhile so my little hip attachment wouldn't feel abandoned because his apprehension over the missing parents was obvious. As we ate, I asked him about his favorite adventures, about sports, school, anything that was a mental diversion.

It was 8:15 by then, so I held his hand and assured him that we'd stay together as long as necessary even if it meant bringing him home with me for the night. No, I was *not* a cougar! Back at the office, I had him write down phone numbers of family, friends and neighbors but all the calls were unsuccessful. To keep him physically and mentally occupied, I asked if he would like to assist me with work. He counted tickets, ran errands for me to Ops and he actually had fun. My fear was that the parents had gotten into a serious accident rendering them powerless to call.

What other possible reasons were there? Only something tragic would have warranted such parental delinquency! Why hadn't any one called? With a heavy heart and mind, I started preparing to be the potential bearer of bad news for this lovable UM. It had been more than six hours with still no communication from the family. How much longer could I wait before implementing a course of action?

Even though we bonded, he was frightened and his anxiety became apparent. The poor guy's voice quivered when he spoke and his legs were jiggling uncontrollably under my desk. Despite his adolescent macho bravado, it became difficult for him to focus. He was visibly shaken up.

Under the guise of wanting sweets, I sent him to the first class lounge to fill up his pockets with goodies. In doing so, it gave me the opportunity to start putting a discerning game plan into action. Just before calling Ops in Germany and beginning the unpleasant process, one last attempt was made to reach his parents. To my surprise, his mother nonchalantly answered the phone. It was such a relief yet my patience were being tested when I asked if she received all the messages I had left on her voicemail re: her distressed son's arrival. I shall never forget her answer…oh, was that today? I did my best to curtail my contempt, but ultimately replied, surely you're not serious! She said that she and her obviously brain-dead husband thought their son was arriving the following day due to the time change.

Had she not confirmed his return date and ETA? The twit told me she forgot about the time difference and actually asked me what it was. I assured her that the universal clock had *not* changed in the last two months and that Europe has always been six hours ahead.

The conversation really got hilarious when I told this award winning mother of the year to be at JFK in 2 hours or her son would be handed over to the proper authorities. When the UM returned with our tray of goodies, I excitedly motioned that his mom was on the phone. He was on the verge of shedding happy tears and we did a few intense high fives. She did not ask to speak to her anguished child and asked if I could check him into a local hotel. The bimbo actually started giving me credit card information, as though I were his aupaire or a front desk receptionist and she assured reimbursement for any costs incurred. What a sport! Since her son was standing next to me, it was really an effort to keep my composure while discreetly cursing her and the preposterous request. She begrudgingly relented and said "well, I guess you leave us no choice but to drive all the way to the airport now", with the emphasis on NOW!

At 12:45 a. m., dumb and dumber finally showed up. The father waited curbside in the car. The bitch of a mother came into the terminal with a surly attitude that I wanted to knock right out of her. As we approached her, she barely embraced her son considering his ordeal and the fact that he was away from home for two months.

Despite breathing a sigh of relief, the emotional anguish and pure physical exhaustion took a toll on him. As this stoic young man ran towards her, he wept, asking repeatedly... where were you? Unfortunately, I had to be civil and could not display my contempt in front of this innocent child, so instead I gave him a big hug, thanked him for his wonderful company, gave him my home number and told him to call me any time for any reason should he have parental issues in the future! I'd like to think this maternally inept woman understood my underlying message and hoped that these morons would never spawn any more babies. I had her sign the UM release and an Incident Report advising her that both will remain on file indefinitely. As I watched them exit the terminal at 1:00 a. m. for a flight that came in at 3:00 p. m., I couldn't help but think how traumatic it had to be for that sweet child and I questioned the quality of his life. That was a first for me and as a mother, it was inconceivable. There was no justification for their despicable parental negligence.

A few days later, I mailed a little package to him consisting of a small model of the aircraft type that he flew in, the airline's official souvenirs......a tee shirt, key chain and pen, along with a "thank you" note for helping me and making that day a very special one and for giving me the opportunity to meet and spend time with such an incredible young man! That was how I wanted him to *remember* the day................. his parents *forgot*!

HAVE A DRINK *ON* ME!

Once upon a time, there was a pretty young maiden who lived on a huge farm in Lancaster, Pennsylvania. She was an only child of German immigrants who adorned their little girl with all the luxuries their hard working hands could provide. Now mind you, the young princess did not lift a finger to help her mommy and daddy. No, that would have been beneath her. She did not *want* to feel the wind in her hair, nor *run* her manicured little fingers through the rich fertile soil, and stepping in cow poop with her Gucci shoes would've been reasons for hysteria. Despite her opulent lifestyle, at twenty one, she had never left the comforts of the farm. When traveling intestate, her mode of transport was the shiny sports car that ma and pa kettle bought for their spoiled little girl.

Aerophobia is a fear of flying. Ironically, there is a correlation between the character in Erica Jong's 1973 iconic novel *Fear of Flying* and our femme fatale in *this* factual story. Both had the need for self-discovery and liberation after being emotionally sheltered for many years. Like any phobias, fear of flight can have serious repercussions if it isn't properly addressed. Aerophobics do not have a fear of the aircraft per se, just the disconnect from solid ground to flight. Fainting, rapid heart rate, nausea, trembling and severe sweating are just a few of the symptoms.

One morning while preparing for the day, I received a phone call from a woman with a heavy German accent advising me that her daughter was a first time flier and that she was extremely nervous about her pending flight that afternoon. Ma was very sweet and apologetic for having burdened me. She asked if the crew could provide a little TLC, given her baby girl's flying apprehension. I told her to have me paged upon check-in and I'd gladly alleviate any of her potential fears. At 2:00 p. m., three hours prior to the departure, she arrived from Lancaster, Pa via a private car service. I prepared a little pep talk for her and had already blocked two bulkhead seats so she'd be comfortable since first-time flying jitters are unnerving.

Upon approaching the counter, I expected to see a German chubby cheeker or a Rebecca of Sunny Brook Farm, pigtails, overalls and all. My jaw dropped when instead, Lolita of Lancaster greeted me with a big smile, a warm hug, and a jar of ma's homemade jam. She was a stunning, sultry beauty with bouncin' and behavin' long black sexy hair..... the *antithesis* of what I had expected. Her clothes were to die for and it was obvious that she was well pampered, no dirt under *her* acrylic nails! Her personality was effusive and a bit naïve as she expressed giddy excitement along with a bit of demur angst.

After checking in, I escorted the pax upstairs to the departure level and requested a brief synopsis of her travel experiences, etc. Well, there weren't *any!* She confessed that she was petrified of flying but was determined to sprout her wings for the first time on our "wings", to visit cousins in Germany. After my pep talk, I excused myself and suggested that since she had three hours until the departure, sipping a glass of wine may perhaps help relax her and that at 3:45 I'd meet her back at the check-in counter to reinforce the pep talk and be done with it. She was very grateful, gave me another hearty hug and off she went to the terminal lounge.

An hour or so later, when I was meeting the inbound flight and waiting for the pax's to deplane, an agent called me on the radio asking if I could come to the counter because a pax was extremely upset and needed to speak with me immediately. When I arrived, there was Lolita, three sheets to the wind and sobbing hysterically. I had very little time to spare but felt since it was my initial *stupid* suggestion that got her shitfaced to begin with, I had to be tolerant. I asked her how many glasses of wine she had. She said, she *didn't* have any wine! Being such a beauty, the bartender happily engaged her in conversation. She revealed her acute fear of flying and he recommended stronger moonshine to calm her nerves. What a swell guy! Three martinis later, her fear of flying intensified. I advised her that it would be in her best interest to offload her luggage and send her back home until she felt comfortable enough to try this again some other time. She wailed at that suggestion and pleaded with me to let her go. Please...I'll sober up, I promise, she repeated in her drunken stupor. It was a tough call because the trip was very important to her, however, based on her inebriated condition, I could not permit her to fly. Fear, alcohol and altitude are not a good mix!

She cried, begged, slobbered all over my uniform, had snot hanging from her nose and it was all *my fault*. The guilt pulled at my heart strings and I foolishly weakened. I read her the riot act about having one hour to completely sober up or it's a no-go! She promised to get a hot meal and have strong coffee. She now cried for joy and said she'd make me proud and would be up at the departure gate on time. Then, more hearty hugs, and again, off she went!

At 4:50 boarding had almost been completed and the agents and I were counting the boarding passes for a gate-check. I thought to myself, that Lolita must have already been o/b, but wondered why she hadn't said goodbye or had she purposely sneaked passed me so I wouldn't deny her boarding again? The count was off by *ONE*. We feverishly recounted several times and sure enough, no gate-check. I ran o/b to see if the little lush was in her seat. She wasn't! Before deplaning, I so hoped to hear the pitter patter of drunken Gucci'ed feet running up the jetway.

Without going off on a tangent, please allow me to stress the importance of being at a departure gate on time. There is so much that gate agents must do before an international flight can leave the gate. It is very frustrating for them and all the other pax's when it is held up because someone chooses to meander and take their time, thinking the captain wouldn't leave without them. WRONG! This holds up the entire a/c and tardy pax's take major risks in having their bags offloaded and their seats given to standbys. Gate agents have the pax's paged several times before re-assigning their seats. For each announcement or page that the airline requests, there is a charge for the PA service. These charges are always passed on to pax's. So, please folks, don't have a cavalier attitude at the airport. Be at your departure gates *on time*! The consequences are not pleasant.

In Lolita's case, my thoughts were that her fear of flying along with the three martinis put her over the top and she split, forfeiting her ticket and purposely leaving her luggage behind for pick up on another day. I had her paged several times to no avail. By then, it was 5:00 p. m. After explaining to the captain why I felt this pax was a no-show, we agreed to have her bags offloaded so he could leave the gate. This procedure can be done relatively fast because the baggage handlers know in which cargo hold everyone's bags are placed. Just then, one of the gate agents came running into the cockpit and said, she's here! We stopped the offloading via radio and I went out to get her. I cringed because she was even more wasted than before. She staggered over to me and started sobbing uncontrollably again...and her breath....Oh my God! I grabbed her elbow, quickly bypassed the purser and sat the little drunk in a bulkhead seat and told her to zip it because the captain would evaluate her condition and then, it was out of my hands.

After buckling her seatbelt, through my teeth, I sternly reiterated, *KEEP YOUR MOUTH SHUT, GOT IT*! Still whimpering, she promised to control herself.

Out comes the slightly perturbed captain from the cockpit. He had every right to be annoyed since we had already taken an unnecessary 15 minute delay. I felt responsible and told him that she's harmless and would fall asleep once the a/c was airborne. He then asked her how much she had to drink. With that, my slurring Lolita became hysterical, shook uncontrollably, bawled like a baby, grabbed both armrests and started screaming, we're going to die, followed by projectile vomiting that landed on *my* knees and on *my* shoes since I was standing in front of her. Need I say what the captain's decision was! While the f/a's angrily cleaned the bulkhead wall from the splattered martini puke, I gagged, sprinted into the a/c toilet, carefully took off my pantyhose, threw them in the tiny disposal and washed the vomit off my knees, legs, and shoes. The baggage handlers had already been instructed to once again remove her luggage STAT. After she cleaned herself off with paper towels, one of the f/a's handed her a barf bag as we left. I apologized for Lolita's hurling and my stupidity.

Even though I encouraged her to have only one glass of wine in lieu of downing six martinis, I made a wrong judgment call and had to face the consequences. Who knew this stunning beauty would be a sloppy lush! We took a forty minute delay because of this fiasco. An agent volunteered to bring her back to the terminal. I booked a hotel room for her near the airport, and called autolink to take her over. My infuriated reaction when she attempted to apologize and hug me was,....Do *Not* come near me! Once she was gone, I then called ma and pa to advise them of her medicinal martini binge and that their sleeping beauty would require transportation and mouthwash in the morning.

I smelled a bit vomity for the remainder of the day and gave my poor shoes the proper burial when I got home. The repercussions for my managerial faux pax that day …....a flight delay, vomit legs, ruined designer shoes and a dumb jar of jam!

A few days later, Lolita tracked me down to apologize. She booked another flight for the following week and asked if I would be there to assist. The little dingbat was serious. I advised her that she wouldn't be accepted on any flights under her current aerophobic condition and proceeded to recommend therapy. I can forgive much of anything, but puking on my shoes was a very, very *bad* thing to do! She had six drinks too many, and literally......all *on* me.

A MIDSUMMER NIGHT'S DREAM

If the traveling public were aware of all the intricacies that are involved in flight operations, it is likely that they would be more amenable with airport staff when distress situations occur. Occasionally, pax's have legitimate gripes, especially when gate agents fail to disclose the basis of a delay. Not informing them simply proliferates their anxieties. It also intimates that they are morons and not worthy of truthful explanations, tantamount to sitting in a doctor's waiting room indefinitely, then getting nondescript answers by a receptionist.. I always encouraged my staff to be honest with pax's because the more they knew, the quieter they were!

An aircraft has several radar systems, one being primary radar and a secondary system called a Transponder. This is an electronic device in the cockpit that transmits signals to and from ATC in providing pressure altitude, positioning and collision avoidance within controlled airspace. There were occasions when an inbound flight would come into JFK with a mechanical problem that was identified by the captain while still airborne. When possible, arrangements and equipment required to rectify issues were made in preparation prior to the a/c's arrival. On one such occasion, while airborne over Bangor, Maine, the inbound captain notified JFK Ops at 1:00 p. m. that the transponder had malfunctioned and needed to be replaced within the two hour allotted ground time.

As mentioned previously, my social life was always in jeopardy because of the nature of the industry. Let's face it, an airline's flight schedule did not conform to Claudia's personal date nights. I accepted this, not graciously at times, but nonetheless, it was a part of my job, yet a bone of contention especially when plans were made that had to be canceled. When receiving the transponder news from the captain, I became seriously despondent, since that night I had an extremely exciting, once in a lifetime social commitment and was determined to go, come hell or high water. That morning, I brought drop-dead gorgeous evening clothes to the airport as I had many times only to be disappointed because of bad flight days that totally ruined my personal plans. So there I was, faced with yet another social crisis because of a stupid transponder. My normal endearing self turned into a cantankerous bitch, flaring nostrils and all, similar to Mayberry's Barnie Fife when Sheriff Taylor purposely roused him. Even though the captain gave me a heads up two hours before the 3:00 p .m. ETA, I went into acute deployment mode and started plotting a fail-proof plan which I implemented immediately. Considering the avionic level of this particular challenge, I wasn't in total denial about incurring a reasonable outbound delay.

Since the airline did not have its own mechanics at JFK, my first frantic call was to our maintenance handler at Delta airlines. After checking, he advised me they didn't have the transponder in stock. He was however, able to get one from Delta maintenance in Atlanta. I did a Lucy Ricardo and shrieked...ATLANTA! That's far away....I need it on the tarmac in two hours and installed within one hour for the 5:00 p. m. departure. He laughed! I cried! After snapping back to reality, I took the mature approach and begged. He put me on hold for several anxiety-prone minutes and came back with good news...a Delta flight was leaving for New York from Atlanta at 1:45. He offered to make arrangements to get it o/b STAT as well as to have it taken off their a/c and deliver it to whomever I sent for the pick up. I was so grateful and expressed my gratitude especially since they had always been reliable in the past. I thought, ok, that was just *too* easy, there had to be a catch. Based on past mechanicals, unforeseen problems didn't always go smoothly. If a certain a/c part was required, getting it was contingent on availability. Fortunately, due to our high a/c maintenance level in Germany, problems were usually an infrequent occurrence. Getting the new transponder to New York was not without its challenges. The thrills and the "Oh SHIT moments had just begun.

The flight from Atlanta was landing at LGA in lieu of JFK. That put a slight crimp on executing my plans in a timely fashion, but nonetheless, it was a minor glitch and with a little nip and tuck, certainly do-able.

My next critical call was to the captain who was flying the a/c back to Germany that evening. He was at the NYC crew hotel getting ready for crew pick-up to JFK. I advised him of the situation and he was thoroughly impressed by my pro-active initiatives especially when I told him a replacement transponder would be rampside in two hours. He asked if this was confirmed and I said *absolutely*! I hung up and had no clue as to how I would do that.

Since I was in the process of hiring an assistant, sending an airline rep to LGA was not an option. I personally could not leave, so my only recourse was to have it picked up. Relying on a delivery service was too risky, thinking they might not be reliable for something so critical …not the transponder, but my pending date! Nor could I trust a stranger to meet with the necessary Delta contact at LGA who was going to personally offload the transponder and hand deliver it to whomever I sent over. No, this had to be placed in someone's hands that was completely responsible, trustworthy and would not require lifelong indebtedness. I thought of the perfect carrier pigeon who had been dependable during our cute courtship a year prior. Even though we remained friends and despite my urgent predicament, it took tenacity to call and ask him. I had nothing to lose and everything to gain. Had he selfishly declined going on this fun field trip for me, my next option was to beg for Divine intervention and barter with a higher up by sacrificing myself to a convent if necessary, after my date of course. Fortunately for me, my friend was home just relaxing. Unfortunately for him, he lived over an hour away from LGA airport and on that hot Saturday afternoon, negotiating the traffic was going to be nasty. He wasn't exactly overjoyed, but agreed to go. We diligently rehearsed all the coordinates and I emphasized, complete with shameless blame, that the responsibility was on his shoulders. For the record, he would be handsomely reimbursed by our airline with a generous Amex gift certificate and two roundtrip tickets to Germany.

Time was of the essence and all was in place....the transponder was airborne and en route to LGA, as was my buddy. The crew was en route to JFK and Delta mechanics were ready with tools in hand. At 3:00 p. m. our handling agents and I were anxiously waiting rampside while the a/c taxied to the hardstand assigned by ATC. The inbound pax's were offloaded via planemates in lieu of a gate.

Pax's are enplaned/deplaned on portside (left.) Ancient mariners docked their ships at "ports" on the left to on/offload crews, otherwise they would have fallen in the water had they exited from the starboard side (right). Since planes are referred to as ships, airports have adhered to this procedure. At most airports, the jetbridges are built to accommodate planes that are aligned facing them, which is another reason why they board and disembark portside. Also, since captains sit in the left hand chair in the cockpit, they have better visual parking access and it's easier for them to monitor wingtip clearances at airports that do not have jetbridges. In addition, basic standard airport traffic patterns are left handed.

Now that you have gained insight into ramp protocol, back at the hardstand, one of our reputable and long-standing handling agents, Triangle Aviation Services, hooked up their mobile truck-mounted stairs on the starboard side which is standard procedure when the a/c is parked at a hardstand. These *remote* stairs allow access to the cabin. I went up into the cockpit to speak with the captain. He had already signed the a/c over to Delta who immediately began removing the faulty transponder.

In the meantime, back at the departure terminal, the agents were busy checking in the pax's. They were unaware of my extraordinary efforts to unselfishly and harmoniously mitigate an on-time departure. (That's funny!) They were happy little clueless faces, oblivious of their pending anguish or of my personal commitment to fulfill one of my "once upon a time" dreams. After returning to the terminal from the tarmac at 3:30 with the a/c in the capable hands of the mechanics, I continued with my usual operational responsibilities and thought to myself, you shrewd little girl, you orchestrated this avionic marvel in record time. After all, it was a "social" emergency!

The flight from Atlanta was due in at 3:45. After landing, Delta would call me, at which point, I would contact my BFF (best friend forever) on his car phone to give him the rendezvous details. The unnerving call from Delta came through on time, and my chivalrous liaison also came through for me. Upon proudly completing his mission, he called to advise that traffic to JFK was at a standstill, so I quickly rerouted him via local side streets, having once lived in Queens for many years. The poor guy was under such pressure, he actually stuttered.

As per the plan, he called me just before he got to our terminal and I ran out to intercept the car. I jumped in and for a fleeting moment, I felt bad. He was sweating and trembling as a result of his three hour traumatic ordeal. With not a second to spare, I just slammed the door shut and said...Thanks...call me! The Holy Grail was finally in my arms at 4:50. High heels and all, I sprinted over people's luggage in the terminal and guarded it as if it were a priceless antiquity. At 5:00 p. m. our handling agent quickly drove it out to the a/c and Delta began the installation. I then raced up to the departure gate where over 300 crazed pax's were anxiously waiting to board the flight that should have already departed. While running en route, the gate agents informed me via radio that they made the appropriate delay announcement. I suggested that they do not disclose the nature of the delay nor a new ETD until Delta assessed the time frame. One hour was the estimated repair time and I set a new ETD for 6:45. Logistically, this gave Delta a one hour and forty five minute window. I was determined to start boarding at 6:00 and have the planemates rampside for enplaning at 6:30. Upon approaching the restless natives at the gate, they encircled me like vultures ready to hang their prey. My immediate thought was to grab the mic and say...just shut up, go sit your asses down and deal with it... at least *You're* all still going to Germany, albeit a bit later than scheduled, but *my* plans for tonight are going down the toilet real quick so suck it up and get over it. But in lieu of that hissy-fit tantrum, my calm announcement consisted of exactly what had transpired all afternoon inclusive of every precise detail so those little ingrates could appreciate all that I had already done to get everyone to Dusseldorf as soon as possible.

At the podium, the usual redundant questions from the pax's began. How much longer,? When are we leaving etc. ? Etc. At 6:00 p. m. the mechanics advised me, they would require yet another thirty minutes and the upsetting update was immediately shared with all the frustrated pax's. Still trying to be optimistic that my social fairytale would come to fruition, perhaps a tad later than foolishly anticipated, I requested three planemates to transport everyone to the a/c out at the hardstand. For those of you who have not thoroughly memorized the glossary, planemates are Port Authority mobile hydraulic vehicles that hook up to the portside a/c doors with a capacity of transporting approximately 125 pax's when a gate is not available. Since they are used by many airlines, it is paramount to secure their usage in advance. When they arrived, we started loading each one as quickly as possible while the pax's bid me a heartfelt farewell. Underneath my gracious smile, my evil thoughts were......no time for idle chit chat, just move it people! The in-flight crew was advised via radio that I was releasing the first one, then the second, then the third. It took thirty minutes to load all three and get them out to the a/c. When they arrived, the purser checked with the mechanics who were still o/b working. Even though Delta required another twenty minutes, she opened the cabin door and advised our handling agent that we could release the planemates for boarding. Since the delay impinged on the crews' flight duty time, they were equally as anxious to depart. With everything in place, our handling agent who was working the flight rampside, drove me out to the aircraft. When we got their, I was incensed that none of the planemates had been offloaded. With panic and nausea, I bolted up the stairs into the cockpit to find out why the crew hadn't allowed the pax to enter the a/c. The captain calmly told me to send them *all back* to the gate indefinitely because there was a problem with the transponder output tube. Everything else he said thereafter became a blur and registered only as blah blah blah.

So there it was, a fiendish communistic plot to decimate my plans for an extraordinary evening and bring it to a sadistic and vicious end! Not only was I devastated, but I knew the pax's would be as well. All three planemates filled with extremely angry people came back to the gate.   My first priority was to go to my office, catch my breath and to get a grip on the cruel realities of the job. Before being fed to the lions, I made the disheartening call to the gentleman who had extended the invitation. My illusions of grandeur again plunged to a record low. Respectfully, I kept him abreast all afternoon of the circumstances,. He encouraged me to keep a positive attitude, but I knew the merciless indefinitely from the captain, was analogous to, *fini,* settle in for the night Claudia! You're not leaving any time soon.

It was miserable enough dealing with the operational issues at hand, but then the planemate operators, who were already narly about waiting for twenty minutes at the hardstand, returned everyone back to the gate and left. They are not required to wait for re-boarding because of the high volume of demand by other airlines. After making my dreaded personal call, I had to bite the bullet and walk directly through the angry mob at the gate to get to the mic. My only recourse was to justify and share their anger, profoundly apologize for the unexpected turn of events and explain to the best of my ability what an output tube was. As stated, pax's listen very attentively because they demand the truth. Once they hear the candid details, they actually do assume a more benevolent attitude. They realize their safety is paramount nor do they want a malfunctioning a/c leaving a minute too soon.

At 8:20 Delta had successfully completed the transponder installation. The planemates were again summoned and I made the final announcement advising the pax's that "It's Time"! While they politely again lined up and walked passed me to reload, I expressed my sincere apology to each one of them.

Delays happen, it's par for the course. We've all been on the other side of the podium. The manner in which a delay is handled becomes crucial for an airline's reputation. After all the planemates were enroute to the a/c, I again went rampside and had a quick briefing with the captain while we waited for the loadsheet. As the planemates emptied out, everyone raced into their seats and our a/c was finally "off the blocks" at 9:00 p. m. As I sat in the car out on the tarmac, the tremendous roar of the engines was exillerating. While waiting for that magnificent aerodynamic marvel to be pushed back, I had to keep my cool to prevent an emotional meltdown when my colleagues expressed genuine remorse for my socially aborted flight of fancy. They knew all too well the commitments and powerful highs and lows that airline staff must endure due to circumstances beyond their control.

In the summer of '93, Pavarotti performed gratis at a Central Park concert. A crowd of 300,000 were estimated to attend. Having been a guest at the 1990 FIFA World Cup Three Tenors concert in Rome three years prior, I was elated to once again be in the presence of greatness. However, my enthusiasm to share spit and sweat with 300,000 strangers was not enchanting. Fortunately, my date knew about this teensy antisocial flaw and made arrangements for us to sit stage-front away from the maddening crowd. Afterward, we were attending a dinner for Pavarotti and friends at Elaine's in NYC. My friend had been a long-time patron of the Metropolitan Opera.

My final curtain call to stoically cancel was at 9:30. While dialing, I clenched down on my lips to keep from crying, calmly cleared my throat to maintain composure and told myself to be cool, don't go into a tizzy. Having anticipated the update, he answered the phone immediately. Like a baby, I started crying and blurted out with juvenile spasmodic eruptions, I can't go, it's not fair, I hate my job, this is so cruel, so on and so forth until I ran out of infantile expletives. My date insisted I just take the helicopter over to NYC *as is,* underline and all, and we'd just meet everyone in the restaurant after the concert. For a fleeting moment, I contemplated it, but by virtue of conventional hygiene, I despairingly declined. I was disheveled, and I stunk from running around all day like a crazed lunatic, trying to execute my perfect plan, in an imperfect world, in an industry where unpredictability was prevalent.

Whenever I had a social commitment in Manhattan, my M.O. was to arrange a comp room at the JFK on-site hotel to shower, do my hair, makeup, change into party clothes, and then take the helicopter to the city. Didn't that seem just so pompous! Well it was. I had many perks as a result of my position.

I was able to work miracles at times, but given that four hour delay, it was logistically impossible. All my life, I always had a Plan B for everything. The alternative to my standard hotel morphing routine was an uncouth sitz bath in an airport sink! As desperate as I was, that was not happening!

In the illusive Shakespearean forest, the euphemistic Puck observed the behavior of its inhabitants… rational/erratic, good/evil, foolish/wise, etc. In his final analysis, he so eloquently concluded "What Fools These Mortals Be"! Without dreams, adventures and passions we merely exist and not fully live.

One of my aspirations was to sing a duet with Pavarotti. My family was raised with classical music and operatic voices were genetic. For weeks prior to the concert, I had become ensconced with fulfilling my midsummer night's dream and visualized myself drinking the bubbly and clinking champagne glasses with the King of the High C's, as we sang "Labiamo", the beautiful drinking song from La Traviata. Because of the transponder tragedy, the only bubbly I experienced that night was from foaming at the mouth and from bubbles that burst and the only party I attended was a pity party.

Having an analytical mind, I had to reconcile this cruel and unjust social deprivation, so I dug deep to understand the silly lesson or the meaningless moral that I was suppose to learn from this unrelenting day. I couldn't come up with much of anything other than, the next time an amazing opportunity presents itself, screw it, I'm going! However, when my eyes dried and my senses returned, I reflected on the extremes that airline staff were subjected to. It surely wasn't financial security, but rather an addictive elixir, distilled with paradoxical passions that set the airline industry apart from the mundane.

Before beginning my work, I stopped by the KLM lounge. (How unusual). My overwhelming sadness was apparent and my colleagues comforted me with generous offerings of verbal and liquid compassion, aka, healing "agents"!

That particular flight day was indeed a compilation of my unfeigned coexisting worlds. Shakespeare's Midsummer Night's Dream imparted relevance to my serendipitous tale from the tarmac, for it begged the question, must we always discern fantasy from reality or can they harmoniously exist? We mortals have become so programmed to deny ourselves a parallel universe. Surviving in an urban jungle infused with all its responsibilities *and* being given an opportunity to sing with Pavarotti were reflections of my essence. The urban jungle had priority that day and with everlasting regret, my visit to the enchanted forest had to remain, an illusive fantasy!

REFLECTIONS
By Ann Mavroudis

I stumbled into the airline industry by chance. Having just finished lunch in Manhattan with an old high school friend, I decided to enjoy the rest of the day by taking a casual walk down Madison Avenue. Although I was not looking for employment, I passed a KLM airline ticket office and meandered in and asked if they were hiring at JFK. The person behind the desk directed me to their personnel office at which point, I was handed an application.

After it was reviewed, they asked if I could go directly to JFK for an interview. Not being prepared for this sudden employment opportunity, I offered to go the following morning. The gentleman who conducted the interview, advised me that the company needed someone who spoke fluent Greek and asked if I would join the training class, already in progress since the prior week. Having lived abroad, I felt right at home being exposed to other worldly cultures and languages. It was an occupational marriage that lasted for thirty-two wonderful years. Over that time, I encountered many challenging and unique experiences. The following vignettes are just a few:

WHEELCHAIR TRILOGY

1) A new agent who was on probation was assigned to wheel an outbound pax to the a/c for departure. Both the agent and the pax were small in stature. As the agent approached a doorway, she feverishly struggled to get the wheelchair across a gaping metal frame. She pushed and pushed when suddenly the fragile gentleman flew out of the chair and onto the floor.

   After her initial shock, she composed herself, picked him up, brushed him off and put him back in the wheelchair, fortunately, not causing him any further injuries.

2) Upon arriving on an inbound flight, one of the pax had requested a wheelchair. Unbeknownst to the arrival agent, the pax was very tall and considerably overweight. The wheelchair that she had brought to the gate.....was not! Even though she realized the chair would be too small, she was determined to squeeze him in. Being embarrassed, he didn't say anything and forced himself down into the chair. When he and the agent reached Customs, his final destination, he struggled to get out, but it was an exercise in futility. As he tried to lift himself up, the wheelchair came with him. It wouldn't leave his behind. After numerous unsuccessful attempts, the agent had to seek additional help to remove him. Two burly men held the chair as the other one pulled him out and "mission accomplished".

3) The distance from the aircraft to Customs and Immigration in the IAT is approximately a twenty minute walk. There are a couple of steep winding ramps that

can be tricky to maneuver when pushing a wheelchair. One of the agents who was a bit inexperienced with the obstacle course, had to transport a pax whose right leg was in a cast from the inbound gate. As she was wheeling him downward, the chair picked up momentum. It sped down the ramp while she hung on and tried to steer it away from an approaching wall. The poor guy had to use the cast on his broken leg to cushion the impact with the wall and bring them to a stop. Neither the cast nor the leg suffered any further injury, however his confidence with the agent and the wheelchair was injured. He decided to walk the rest of the way to Immigration, limping all the way!

UNDER THE INFLUENCE
By Ann Mavroudis

Airport staff must be prepared for adversity on a daily basis. With occasional exceptions, inebriated pax tend to be harmless. Alcohol has a way of bringing out the best or the worst in people. Such was the case when an employee had to call a supervisor over during an outbound departure to Amsterdam. A drunk pax from another airline that had been denied boarding demanded on getting on the KLM fl ight. The supervisor tried to calm this irate pax. His behavior quickly escalated from verbal to physical abuse. Without warning, this large, intimidating person pushed her so hard that she landed on the other side of the floor hitting her head against the wall. The Port Authority police were immediately summoned, but he disappeared. PA police and security were able to track his alternate departure plan from another city. They had his itinerary and he was followed very closely by all. Upon his return to the U.S., the KLM supervisor, security and the PA police were waiting to greet the jerk on the jetbridge, at which point he was handcuffed and arrested for assault. Moral of the story…While under the influence don't mess with JFK staff!

THE OSTRICH FLIGHT
By John Grasser

In the mid nineties, employed as Station Manager at JFK for a major European airline I was able to get myself caught up in a feathered frenzy that shall remain with me until they throw dirt on the coffin. I should start off by saying that we flew Boeing 747 combi aircraft into JFK in those days. A combi is an aircraft configured to carry passengers as well as cargo on the main-deck, separated by a wall. Because this area was heated the same as the passenger cabin, and offering about 100 inches of height for shipments, 96 inches to be exact, if you care, we were able to move very large animals, such as horses, chimps, and the like, which was a very lucrative market for our cargo division. We even fl ew in a shark once, but that's another story.

Well, one extremely cold winter day I received information on a high value shipment of baby ostriches that were due to arrive in a few days. If I recall correctly the number was 150, with 25 per crate. They were coming from Africa, transferring through Amsterdam, into New York. Now, we were constantly shipping baby chicks (chickens) and they were known to be quite sensitive to extreme temperatures.

If it was too warm, they would perish due to the heat and if it was too cold they would freeze to death if exposed to the weather for any extended period of time. That meant the shipper would place a claim against our cargo department, and in turn cargo would moan to me about crappy handling and not caring about their product, blah, blah, blah,. You got the idea, right.

The week the ostriches were scheduled to arrive was one of the coldest we had experienced in a long time. So cold in fact, that there were a few flights that had to return back to Europe with the inbound freight because the cargo door was frozen shut and could not be opened upon arrival. I'm talking low teens, single digits here in NY. Now, with my vast experience in dealing with baby chickens, and knowing quite well about the high value of these ostrich chicks, I made the educated decision to delay them. After all, they were coming from Africa and must be protected against the cold at all costs. So I telexed (no e-mail back in the day) Amsterdam to hold the ostriches until I advised further before I left the airport for the day.

Returning to work the next morning I received a rather long, wordy telex (remember, no e-mail) from none other than our Senior Vice President of Operations advising me that under no conditions should the ostriches be delayed further. They were insured for a million dollars, the consignee in the States was screaming that he needed the birds, and a law suit was pending. He added that he didn't care how we got the birds into NY and off of the aircraft but we better get it done. And for a kicker, it was noted that the birds were growing at a rate of 3 inches per day! Growing at 3 inches a day! I now had this cartoon vision of these poor birds with their little heads and little legs sticking out of the crate, growing larger by the hour, and it was all my fault.

So, based on this love note from our Sr. VP I had no option other than to have the shipment flown into JFK and offloaded into sub 20 degree weather. Calls were placed to our cargo department to make sure the consignee was advised and ready to accept his damned ostriches. Plans were readied, pre-meetings were conducted. All equipment was checked and in place. In such cases, specialized 16 wheelers are used to load shipments directly from the aircraft on the tarmac. They are equipped with rollers that are hydraulically raised and lowered to allow the shipment to easily roll on and off the trucks, but more on that later. I must add that the trucks were the responsibility of the consignee.

The time has come, the flight is heading west, coming across the Atlantic, our cargo department has brought the consignee over to the ramp with his two trucks, a meeting is held. I find out that ostrich is the new beef, very lean and tasty, easy to raise and I should be seeing it in supermarkets in the not too distant future. Sure thing, I think to myself', all I want to do is get these birds the hell off of my aircraft without flash freezing them. We close the meeting in full agreement. The flight will arrive, the high loader will be positioned at the main deck door, the trucks will position, and the birds will be offloaded. As Ed Norton, chef of the future. once told TV viewers, zip, zip, it is done. We leave the office, me in silent prayer that the cargo door will not be frozen shut upon arrival.

The new ostrich rancher has brought along pallet plastic to wrap around the crates in an attempt to protect the birds from freezing winds, and the bitter cold, a good idea

I thought to myself! I try to size up the fellow a bit prior to the flight arriving. He looks like he is ready to have a nervous breakdown and seems to know very little about the birds he has most likely spent his life savings on by having them shipped in from Africa. Oh well, it's the new beef, he'll be fine.

The circus begins. The aircraft arrives at the gate, the passengers start to deplane. We hold our breath until the cargo door begins to open. Step one is a success, the door opens, I breath a sigh of relief. Little did I know that would be the last time I would breath normally for the next hour, actually many hours afterward. Have you ever wondered what 150 ostriches that have been penned up in crates for about 5 days smell like! I have been involved in the shipment of a good number of odorous shipments before. I have been subjected to the smells of horse shit, cattle shit, monkey shit*, mink shit, dog shit, cat shit and an array of other shits. This shit took the cake, I wouldn't wish this smell on Osama Bin Laden, well, maybe him. I stopped breathing up there on the main deck. The thought of that ostrich shit air entering my lungs was sickening. My scarf immediately went over my mouth and nose. *Side note…did you know that monkeys will throw their shit at you? Be forewarned.

The ostrich rancher is on the main deck, feverishly wrapping the crates in plastic in preparation for offload. The first two pallets of birds are on the loader, being lowered to the truck that had been positioned. The first pallet starts to enter the truck, but there is a problem. Remember those hydraulically controlled rollers that are raised in the truck bed to make it an easy on load ? From what I witness, it looks as if they are not working but this is not the first time such a situation has presented itself. There is a procedure that can work, although not recommended for live shipments, but we have no choice. What takes place is that the first pallet is positioned at the truck doorway and then forced into the truck by the second pallet which is being moved along by the loader, also hydraulically operated. All goes well, pallet one is in place. Now comes number two which of course, presents problems as it can not be fully forced into the truck. So, the second pallet is partially forced in and the truck slowly pulls away from the loader. Again, there is a procedure I have seen used on the ramp that has always made me cringe when initiated, and this time, it's with million dollar birds. I need to add that at this point I am back down on the ramp, watching intently and trying to breath normally. The procedure that follows is that the truck driver slowly speeds up (remember that slowly word) and then brakes hard, which in turn "jerks" the pallets into the truck. One attempt works a bit, the second attempt, a bit more. Now, on the third attempt the driver must have realized how to operate the hydro wheels and raises them. But this time he elects to "gun" it forward, which in turn starts the two pallets of birds to roll backwards, out of the truck ! In all honesty, that second pallet was more than half way out of the truck, bent almost to the ground before that jackass hits his brakes and it catapults back into the truck. At that point I am not sure if I was frozen due to the weather or out of fear for my life when that pallet started heading out of the truck in my direction. I also thought at that moment I might experience a new smell, that of ostrich rancher shit. Once that dumb ass trucker figured out how to operate the rollers, the other pallets were easily loaded onto the trucks and driven away.

The shipment is loaded and leaving the field, the rancher looks totally exhausted from the ordeal, the cargo manager seems pleased it went OK (ha,ha,ha) and I am just happy to have it over and done with. We all say good-bye and get on with our tasks, but I have one minor problem. My clothes, my shoes, my hair and everything about me smells like ostrich shit. I can't shake it, I reek. Thank goodness this was the last flight of the night for us, I can go home and sand blast myself. I end up having to leave my clothes out in the garage for a good week until I can even take them to the cleaners. The next day when I arrive to work there is another telex from our Sr. VP congratulating me on the good job. I start thinking,,,, well, I'd better keep that thought to myself.

As I mentioned at the start of this story, that was the mid nineties, and we are now closing in on 2010. Allow me to ask, when is that last time you saw an ostrich steak offered for sale in the meat section of your local supermarket? I did find it once or twice on a few restaurant menus, but I could never get myself to order one because more than likely I knew that poor steaks grandfather.

One final point. Years later on an aircraft as a passenger I was thumbing through a magazine and came upon an advertisement for ostrich farming. There was a picture of a few of those dopey looking birds standing in some pen in Colorado or someplace like that. What really caught my eye was that they were standing in about two inches of snow. It must have been pretty cold where they were. Go figure.

THE SHANNON FLIGHT
By Dennis Wrynn

Flight 876 was a daily Boeing 707 from the TWA Flight Center at JFK, to Shannon, Ireland. From the perspective of a PRR (TWA Passenger Relations Representative) it was an easy flight to work. The vast majority of pax's were lovable Irish-Americans vacationing in the "old country". The flight terminated in Shannon and connecting pax's were rare. In the case of a flight delay, if there were "miscons", few if any, needed assistance. The practice of issuing food and beverage vouchers for use in the flight center bar and restaurant was usually received joyously by the delayed pax's and rarely did any incidents occur.

That being said, I was the PRR in Wing 11 assigned to 876 on a given Saturday night when the 8:00 p. m. departure time was delayed due to a mechanical problem with the a/c. The agent handling the flight distributed the vouchers to all the pax's and informed them that the new ETD was at 9:00 p. m. All the happy little people headed for the bar.... what a shocker! There was however, one exception.....a rather short, middle-aged man who loitered near the emptied gate area. He started haranguing me about the delay, TWA and my parentage, which he considered dubious. He had an Irish surname and proceeded to inform me that he was a medical doctor in Terre Haute, IN. The good medico finally wandered unsteadily off towards the bar, apparently *already* under the influence.

The cheerful pax's drifted back to the gate at 8:45 and since the mechanical had been resolved, boarding began immediately. The gate agent did an onboard headcount and reported one pax missing. Knowing right away who it was, I made a final terminal-wide departure announcement while the agent walked halfway down the connector tunnel to make sure there wasn't a "runner". As planned, the flight broke the gate at the new departure time. Twenty minutes later, the missing pax staggered into the gate area and bitterly accused me of not making the proper departure announcement, to which I replied that 117 other pax's had obviously gotten the word. He then demanded that the flight be recalled for him.....of course, it was not.

Our traveler was very irate, very drunk and shouted derogatory remarks, threats, and obscenities as I stood sideways in front of him in case he attempted to kick me.

The doctor was most unsteady on his feet and his back and forth rocking motion increased perceptibly with each sway. I realized that he would either pitch forward into me or pitch backwards onto the hard tile floor. By this time, I was pretty angry myself and obviously had a decision to make regarding this fool's immediate future. So, I simply decided to let the Gods make the choice for me....and they did. It was not a pretty picture as he hit the floor with a severe blow, splitting his scalp open causing profuse bleeding. The Port Authority police were called and they hauled the wounded drunkard away to the nearby Jamaica Hospital (not a good destination.)

My scheduled days off were Sunday and Monday, so I thought it best to submit an "Irregularity Report" to the shift supervisor and the station manager explaining the incident. Sure enough, when I reported for work on Tuesday, the station manager called me into his office. The pax had shown up on Monday morning with a bandaged head and vehemently accused me, "the big guy with the moustache" of purposely knocking him down and then stealing his wallet. John Murphy threw him out of his office!

A TRIP TO IRELAND
By Dennis Wrynn

During the 1960's, several of the international carriers operating out of JFK would offer periodic "fam" trips (familiarization trips to the employees of domestic carriers at little or no cost.) The purported justification for these trips was to foster good relations between employees of the sponsoring airline and the invited domestic airline personnel. This would hopefully lead to "special consideration" at the expense of the competition, be it domestic or int'l. when booking or re-booking connecting pax's. That rationale had some validity to it, however, interline trips were usually one big party from beginning to end with very happy people. The jaunt would normally be of three to four days duration and include about twenty airline employees plus a tour leader from the host airline. Sight-seeing, dining and drinking, not necessarily in that order, were on the schedule.

Aer Lingus offered a number of these trips each year, usually to Shannon and the West of Ireland and they were often accompanied by Christie Ryan, the charismatic station manager for Aer Lingus. The excursion would begin in the airline's First Class Lounge where the eagerness to begin the adventure was contagious, with much banter and laughter amongst the trip members getting to know each other. However, on one of these memorable fam trips, the jollity in the lounge was marred by the sudden outbreak of tears from a female participant named Jeannie. The young lady in question had forgotten her passport at home. She knew she could no longer go on the trip. The joyous atmosphere at the bar quickly dissipated and everyone was rather depressed by this turn of events. Comforting the inconsolable Jeannie was to no avail as she gathered her belongings ready to head home with a heavy heart.

Just then, Christie Ryan entered the conversation and asked Jeannie if she knew anyone who could bring the passport to the Aer Lingus departure terminal in time for the following night's flight to Shannon. She replied in the affirmative: **YES** and that her sister could do it. Ryan put his arm around her and happily informed her that the problem was solved and that she wouldn't need her passport to enter Ireland. He told her she would only need it to get back into the U.S. and barring any difficulties, the document would catch up with her in Ireland long before it was time to fly back home.

The partying aura returned immediately by all and another round of drinks were ordered. When pressed about the legality of this passport maneuver, Ryan replied that it didn't matter, as his cousin was in charge of Customs at Shannon and the two of them would take care of the details. A great time was had by all, especially Jeannie.

KEEPING COOL IN A CRISIS, LEGAL OR OTHERWISE

By Dennis Wrynn

The importation of illegal drugs into the US via air, sometimes with the unfortunate connivance of airline employees, was an increasingly difficult problem during the late 1960s, and both airline security personnel and US Customs officials were heavily involved in attempting to disrupt and destroy these illicit operations.

There was a story circulating at JFK which involved Pan Am personnel attempting to smuggle heroin into the United States. Allegedly, the drugs were given to a Pan Am flight attendant by the supplier at departure from a Caribbean airport. Upon landing at JFK, the F/A would turn the heroin over to a Pan Am ramp agent who met the aircraft, and in turn would transport the drugs out of the customs area in a company vehicle which was not subject to a customs inspection. In this instance, the ramp agent informed the arriving courier that he could not take the drug package, as US Customs was aware of the impending transfer and he was being closely watched. At this point the F/A must have been close to panicking, but apparently she handled the situation very well, even legally.

Aircraft crews arriving from overseas re-entered the US through the ship's office at the International Arrivals Building at JFK. Until they had done so, the crews were in limbo, not yet legally in the United States. When asked by the customs agent in the ship's office if she had anything to declare, the flight attendant drug courier replied in the affirmative, saying she had five pounds of heroin to declare. When told that it was illegal to bring heroin into the US, she complied by dumping the package in a trash barrel. As she had not entered the country with the illegal substance, US Customs had no choice but to let her proceed and took no action against her. It was said that Pan Am fired the flight attendant due to this incident but she certainly ducked a federal bullet and certainly, she ducked jail time!

IRATE "IAB" IMBECILE
By Dennis Wrynn

During the early 1970's, the IAB (International Arrivals Building..... today known as the IAT, International Arrivals Terminal) at JFK was a fascinating place to work and from which to observe the world. Until TWA and Pan Am moved their arrivals facilities into their own terminals, every arriving international flight disembarked at the IAB and every airline maintained a ticket counter in the main lobby to assist both arriving and connecting pax's.

Thousands of weary pax's arrived daily at the IAB during peak travel periods and were often met by thousands more, usually family and friends. The airline personnel at the IAB were surrounded by a sea of humanity every day. Some arrived drunk, some happy, some angry. Many were confused and terrified of the NY airport system. Among the arrivals, there would routinely be "misconnects" and "arunks" (arrival unknown) seeking domestic flight connections as well as pax's with a variety of problems and questions, thus the need for maintaining airline counters in the arrivals hall lobby.

The airline staffs put up with much harassment and unwarranted insults, but in general, they handled these pax's with self-confidence as a result of their vast experience in the realm of air travel. The employees were a most interesting collection of people from all over the world, of every ethnicity, every race, religion, and sexual orientation. All in all, they were a fabulous group to associate with on a daily basis. Many of them were legendary characters, and were a lot more fun than the United Nations crowd in NYC.

One day, a situation arose between a British Airways agent named George and an angry, most likely drunk-on-arrival pax. He approached the BA ticket counter demanding a message he was expecting to receive upon arrival. But after George carefully searched the counter, he politely advised the pax that there was **no** message for him. The irate man started shouting, calling George several uncomplimentary names and demanded that he again look for the missive. The SOP was to page the arriving pax's with messages as their flights passed through the US Customs and Immigration area. George of course knew this, but to mollify the angry pax, he went into a small office behind the ticket counter to check if by chance there was indeed a message left on the desk or the bulletin board. Once again, George had to inform him, that there was **no** message. The pax went into a loud tirade, slammed his fist on the counter and made an utter fool of himself. He simply refused to take **no** for an answer.

Airline ticket counters are usually chest-high to form a barrier between the pax's and the agent for the purpose of protecting employees from physical attacks by customers.........we've all seen it happen. George was quite short, perhaps 5' 2" in height. After dealing with this jerk who refused to accept

"no message", he looked the pax square in the eye and said that there was one other place where the message might be: he would look "downstairs". With a perfectly straight face, George pantomimed going down a flight of steps behind the counter to a make-believe office, with his head slipping lower and lower until he disappeared from the pax's line of sight. We heard his shoes clumping on every alleged step. Crouching on the floor, George started throwing papers, schedules and pax manifests high in the air, all the time shouting from his spot on the floor..."sorry, there doesn't seem to be any message for you from "downstairs" either". He then turned himself around to face the other direction and again with the same straight face, he re-emerged from the non-existent office.....his head and body rising one step at a time.

Several of us who were working the counters next to him watched this brilliant performance. We were in total hysterics. I think at that point the pax realized he had been duped as his face reddened while he calmly thanked George for his help and swiftly left the building, never looking back!

LOOK!...........UP IN THE SKY
........IT'S A BIRD!
By P.D.B.

As an Aerospace engineer retiree, I would like to share the following true stories regarding seagulls congregating on the airfield at our Long Island facility. I hope you will find them as amusing today as they were back then. In a frantic attempt to rid the airfield and the runways of this dangerous problem, the airport manager purchased a device which he thought would be a sure-fire fix.

Birds flying into aircraft windshields and engines have been a problem since the Wright Brothers.....case in point, Captain Sullenberger's heroic landing on The Hudson River last January as a result of a flock of birds that shut down both engines on the USAir flight while airborne over New York.

We all tried to find solutions to this ongoing problem in our Engineering Dept. since our fighter aircrafts were constantly being bombarded with the birds and their poop! Subsequently, this caused major damage to the cockpit canopy. When addressing this issue at meetings, the birds became known as **UFFF's...** *Unidentified Foul Flying Fowls.* The ingenuity and the wisdom of the "egghead" dept. decided to construct an "air cannon" to shoot chickens that were approximately the size of the **UFFF's.** The brilliant idea was met with rousing approval by all. Keeping in the avian spirit, a gaggle (pardon the pun) of eager engineers descended upon local butcher shops to purchase chickens, deceased and plucked! Upon delivery of this new miracle air cannon device, I assigned people to install this said device on the runway. Several days later, upon inspection, I went out to the airfield to see this gadget in operation. The big day arrived! With the integrity of the windshield ready to be tested, the chickens...locked and loaded and.....PFFFFFFFFFFFFT BOOOM! The featherless missiles with nary a miss, struck with devastating results. The cheers and proud back-slapping moments were soon to be halted. Unbeknownst to these gallant cannonized intellectuals, mangled chicken parts from the test firing graced front porch railings, eaves and roofs of neighboring houses and splattered all over mid Island. Needless to say, this half-baked UFFF project found its way to the "dead file" bin real quick!

Shortly after the cannon fiasco flop, a frantic second attempt was made to rid the airfield of the UFFF's. After the initial humiliation of the cannon debauchery wore off and subsequent research from a different viewpoint, the airport manager and a team of eggheads went out to Eastern Long Island to visit a farmer who had invented a gadget that prevented crows from feasting on his harvest. For all intended purposes, this gizmo was a sure-fire fix! Once again, the same cannon cohorts installed it with convinced certainty that the UFFF airfield problem would be resolved by ridding them from the ground.

I must first describe it.....picture if you will, a two foot long aluminum tube with a fourteen inch propeller attached to one end and a ten inch propeller on the other end mounted on stanchions by the side of the runway. The object being, that one prop would spin clockwise while the other, counter clockwise. I can only say that after looking at this "toy", I burst into a fit of laughter. Fortunately, I didn't lend credence or my name to this engineering marvel. Once in operation, the seagulls reacted immediately....not by flying away, but by nonchalantly sitting under the convoluted contraption, just chilling out! To add insult to injury, they were enjoying the cool breeze and the soft "*whirrrs*" as the props gently lulled the happy little seagulls to sleep. If they could talk, the UFFF's would have requested a dozen more!

Proving to be totally useless, it was removed a few days later and added to the dead file bin along with the cannon. Both avianic projects "flew the coup"!

DO AS I SAY......NOT AS I DO
By Gerry Moore

So here I am, one frigid, routine morning in 1965 on my way to Heathrow for an 0700 shift. I was tootling along the airport road in my battered, sputtering old Morris Minor, half daydreaming and thinking of nothing in particular. The only notable event on my shift was the scheduled arrival of a Boeing 707 charter from New York at 0730, and I was the only Aer Lingus staff member on duty covering that arrival. It was 0645, and I was almost there when Lo and behold, I saw a big Aer Lingus Boeing 707 taxiing across one of the airport overpasses – fully 45 minutes early. Shit, shit shit I remember saying to myself as I raced to the office. I found out that the aircraft had been assigned a hardstand (remote parking) assignment, so I grabbed the keys of a ramp car and drove like the clappers to get there, hopefully before the aircraft did. I got there just as it was being marshaled to its parking position. (No jetways then folks – just ramp buses to take the passengers to the terminal).

Engines shut down, the signal was given to position the stairs to the front passenger door and the first bus pulled up to the foot of the stairs. I saw then to my horror, that the ground between the bottom step and the bus was a sheet of ice – obviously a hazard to passengers and a potential lawsuit if any of them slipped and got hurt.

Quick as a flash, I signaled the cabin crew to hold the passengers while I went up the steps to make an announcement asking the passengers to be careful as they boarded the bus due to ice on the ramp. They waited patiently for my announcement and, on my instructions, followed me down the steps. With a whole planeload of passengers watching and following my instructions, I stepped off the bottom step and fell right on my ass on the ice – losing my uniform cap in the process, to the cheers of the delighted passengers., Mortified, I picked myself up and went to retrieve my cap, which by now was blowing across the ramp, completely forgetting of course, about the ice. Another resounding cheer went up from the delighted passengers, as I went down to the ground for the second time.

No further announcements were even contemplated……

NEXT OF KIM
by Harry Gegner

One morning, when KLM was servicing the Caribbean on a daily basis, we were holding our flight for a large group of Korean merchant seamen in transit from Korea to Curacao. Once the group arrived, all TRWOV'S (transits without visas) had to be checked in. This was not an easy task to accomplish in a short period of time.

The KLM agent called the first passenger whose surname was KIM. Simultaneously, *all* of the seamen got up and came to the counter at once. A bit bewildered by the stampede of passengers, the agent once again called for passenger KIM *only* to approach the counter! All hands went up in the air... "everybody KIM"...they said. Little did we know that we literally had fifty-five KIMS on that pending flight. From what we surmised, KIM was a very common name in Korea. Our computers were programmed in a way that by getting one KIM's boarding pass, we were able to retrieve all fifty-five at once which enabled our KLM flight to have an on-time departure.

Years later, we handled KAL (Korean Airlines) and found out that on every Korean flight, there were seventy KIM's, sixty PARKS, and fifty LEE's. The flight manifests looked like perpetual typographical errors. As a result, every pax had to be checked in using their first name, *then* their surname, which is contrary to the universal check-in procedure. Either the redundancy of the name has a long-standing ancestral lineage or there's some serious hanky-panky going on in Korea!

LOST AND FOUND
By Rosa Kamel

My name is Rosa Kamel. At the ripe old age of eighteen and just out of high school, I had been told from a friend of mine that *Air France, or as we* we jokingly called it... *Air Chance,* was hiring temporary summer passenger service employees. I was lucky enough to be hired even though I did not speak a word of French at the time. This temporary summer job, turned into a full time experience that lasted approximately seven years. I had many interesting and exciting experiences while working at JFK.

I shall never forget one experience in particular. We handled an airline called Air Afrique. Upon arrival of all Air Afrique flights, and all international carriers per se, one of the not-so -fun duties of a passenger service agent was to clear any suitcases and packages that were not claimed by the arriving passenger. The reasons being were that passengers would legitimately forget to pick them up in the excitement of coming into the USA or, they knew they were bringing in something illegal and felt at the proverbial eleventh hour, they were going to get caught. Well, that morning, was indeed one of those flights where the latter applied! Approximately a dozen bags were unclaimed leftovers.

In clearing the left over baggage, we first had to get them opened with master keys for the various locks that these suitcases might have had. If that didn't work, we just clipped the locks off, so Customs and Immigration could view the contents. Well, on this particular 5 a. m. arrival, after the sixth or seventh suitcase, the routine process of opening them continued. They contained the usual dirty laundry, while some contained interesting items such as African wood carvings, Ivory elephant tusks (illegal of course) and other bizarre things that just never ceased to amaze me. With each one I opened, my thoughts were, one man's gold is another man's junk and how true that was! I came to one suitcase that had some tears all around it and it looked pretty beat up. Although its exterior appearance seemed a bit odd, I nonetheless, had to get it open. As I carefully unzipped the suitcase and flipped the top open, I almost went into cardiac arrest. All I saw was a huge open mouth with very large teeth that instantly snapped at me. It was a baby alligator! My screams were heard throughout the building. Custom and Immigration officers came racing over to me as the alligator started crawling out of the suitcase. I stood there in total disbelief! Luckily, thanks to a quick thinking janitor, he carefully put a big empty garbage pail over it and subsequently dazed the new JFK arrival, until quarantine officers came and nabbed the African gator and took it to the JFK quarantine facilities. The passenger never did return to claim his friend, with the fear of being fined and arrested for bringing in a live and dangerous animal without proper documentation...'ya think! I don't know what happened to the baby gator, who by now must be fully grown and probably swimming in our Florida lakes.

Normal procedure back then was that plain old unclaimed bags filled with dirty laundry were held for three months and then simply disposed of. The holding area was not a place you wanted to be in any longer than necessary. If anything of major value was found, it was reported to Port Authority. That storage facility must be quite interesting, and where does the "stuff" go after the three months...to the eternal lost & found abyss? My experiences such as this one, definitely made coming to work every day, unique and exciting. It earned its annuls in JFK's history of Tales From The Tarmac!

HIJACKING OF PAN AM FLIGHT 93

By Ursula Goeschen

As mentioned in my Dedication, my friend Ursula, who worked at Pan Am's Worldport at JFK had been a Special Service Supervisor prior to her position with LTU. One day, while managing the usual pax related nuances, she was advised, along with the limited details, that a Pan Am 747 a/c had just been hijacked. Back then, disseminating information was much slower than it is today, thanks to the ever-evolving high tech world, which makes media news readily available as it unfolds. She immediately began coordinating and processing incoming data to the proper system channels worldwide.

The hunger for peace in the Middle East has always been untenable. As a result, a number of political and military organizations were founded under the guise of equality. On Sept. 6th, 1970, members of a Palestinian terrorist group hijacked four jet a/c's, all bound for New York. Their successful mission statement was to get Palestinian guerillas released from European and Israeli prisons. The first two, a TWA flight from Frankfurt, and a Swissair flight from Zurich, were ordered at gunpoint to land at Dawson's Field, an abandoned British Royal Air Force airstrip in the Jordanian desert.

The third was an EL AL flight which originated in Tel Aviv with a stop in Amsterdam then onto to JFK. This too was commandeered to land at Dawson's Field. To execute this well-rehearsed take-over, four terrorists were to board EL AL's Fl. 219 together, but only two got through security. Approximately half hour into the flight while over the British Isles with the hijacking already in progress, the flight attendants refused to open the cockpit door. Immediately after he was advised via an intercom, the captain put the a/c in negative-G mode which caused a sudden drop in altitude. He intentionally made a steep nosedive so the two hijackers would lose their balance and fall. Subsequently, the sky marshal killed one of them and with the help of pax's, he seriously wounded the other. A safe emergency landing was made at London's Heathrow airport.

The fourth was a Pan Am aircraft. This hijacking took place because that afternoon, when all four originally checked in for the El Al flight, two of the four terrorists were denied boarding at Schiphol Airport in Amsterdam. Their counterfeit African passports had sequential numbers and that raised the red flag. The other two were cleared. The two that *were* bumped, one being an American citizen, decided to hijack Pan Am flight 93 instead.

Aircraft hijackings were easily plotted back then because airport security and screening were still in their infancy stages. Up until 9/11, weapons were simply concealed and carried onto an a/c.

The Pan Am flight originated in Brussels with a stop in Amsterdam en route to its home at JFK. While on the runway and ready for take-off, the captain brought the a/c to an abrupt stop. He was suspicious about the two African passport holders and engaged them in conversation. Shortly afterward, the hijackers seized the a/c instructing the crew to head for Jordan. The quick-witted captain convinced the terrorist that he could not land at Dawson's Field because the new Pan Am 747 jumbo jet was too large for that airstrip. He flew to Beirut for refueling at which time, several more hijackers boarded with additional explosives. From there it was commandeered to Cairo, Egypt where these savages had one of their headquarters. At 4:30 a.m. just before touchdown, one of the grenades had already been lit. The pax's and crew were told by the hijackers that they had to exit the a/c immediately because within three minutes, all the explosives would detonate. According to reports, the in-flight director (hero of that flight) and the crew deployed the emergency chute and safely evacuated all 136 pax's in one and half minutes...the fastest ever in emergency landings. The a/c was out on the tarmac with no access to safety and everyone ran, leaving their belongings behind. Within one minute of escaping onto the tarmac, they watched in horror as the 747 exploded and burst into flames.

Once they were taken care of, Pan Am ferried a Rome/ Cairo aircraft to bring them back home. Ursula, along with her colleagues, made the necessary distressed arrival arrangements. She called a local department store by the name of Bargaintown advising them that she and a coworker would be there shortly to purchase amenities for 136 pax's. Since the flight was arriving on a late Sunday afternoon, that was the only store still open. They advised her that the doors would be closing soon. Ursula then spoke to the manager and asked him to please understand the tragic nature of the situation, and he then complied. They bought every pair of shoes, every pair of slippers and anything else that resembled shoes since the pax's all came in empty handed and barefooted. When they evacuated the a/c in Cairo two days prior via the emergency chute, standard procedure mandated removing their shoes. The Pan Am staff feverishly assembled 136 goodie bags (amenities, shoes etc.). Upon meeting the flight, they were handed out to everyone as they exited the a/c. Ursula vividly recalled how dazed, yet amazingly calm the pax's were...until one little girl, approximately four years old started crying and despairingly started looking for her doll. *That* was the breaking point for everyone!

On Sept. 8th, the pax's whose final destination had been Los Angeles and various other U.S. cities, were reconnected on flights and were given first class seating. That day, they had once again been traumatized. Forty eight hours later, while looking out the window, yet another aircraft burst into flames for the second time in front of their eyes!

A Trans International Airlines DC-8 was deadheading from JFK to Dulles Airport in Virginia. At take-off from runway 13R, he climbed to 300 ft., rolled to the left, crashed and caught fire, killing all eleven crew members o/b. According to reports, a piece of asphalt debris had entrapped itself in the aft stabilizer which is on the tail of the a/c and provides stability.

On Sept. 9th, a fifth plane, BOAC, pre-cursor to British Airways flight from Bombay to London was hijacked. The terrorists plotted yet another empowering demand, i.e., the release of the female hijacker who was wounded on the foiled EL AL hijacking and arrested upon the emergency landing at Heathrow. The a/c also was permitted to refuel in Beirut and then commandeered to Dawson's Field to join TWA and on Sept. 11, the majority of hostages were released, with the exception of flight crews and fifty six Jewish pax's. On Sept. 12, all three empty a/c's were blown up with explosives. On Sept. 30th, the remaining hostages were freed. The various governments acceded to the hijackers demands which eventually afforded them carte blanche to execute more grandiose acts of terrorism.

Hijacking was a viable tool to stimulate publicity and gain recognition for a particular cause. This form of submersion eventually became child's play and transitioned from a political tool to a murderous weapon.

For Ursula and her colleagues, Sept. 8th's afternoon, morphed into Sept 9th's morning and continued indefinitely with no respite for the weary staff. Compassion cannot be measured in linear time. The staff humbly gave of themselves for they knew their workload was so inconsequential in comparison to the terror and the anguish those brave pax's endured on Pan Am's frightful Flight 93.

AIRLINE ADDICTION
By John Mangano

Many people start out in other careers, but once they enter the airline business they become trapped with a lifelong addiction. Working "the line" is very much like being in a love affair that involves extreme highs and painful lows. For those who are not members of this great family they will never truly be able to understand that this "love" becomes an eternal partner.

I started out as a New York City Iron Worker. My job entailed "walking steel" sixty stories in the air with some of the best and bravest people you could find. You and your partner would work in tandem…each pinning his end of the beam with nuts and bolts and then walking the beam high above the clouds to the next one.

One job I will always remember was installing the windows on the World Trade Center 110 stories high in the sky…you could easily see JFK Airport from that spot high above New York City.

One day, I got a call from a friend of mine who was the Station Manager of North East Airlines at JFK. They were having problems with their new computer cargo moving equipment they were looking to contract on a permanent basis. He asked me if I knew anything about that type of equipment and if I could help him out. I told him that "if it has a blueprint, the location is on the ground and its warm…I'm your man!" He hired me on a trial basis as a consultant.

I got the shock of my life as I quickly found out that the cargo airline business at JFK was the Las Vegas of the East… sin, sex, and shoddy work all entangled within a strong labor union. However, from the viewpoint of a strong, young, iron worker who would try anything and didn't know fear…this sounded like an ideal assignment.

My first day at JFK I drove out in my shiny Buick Rivera to meet with the airline Cargo Director and his staff. The guard at the facility told me if I want to park close to the cargo building I would have to pay a fee…strange I thought since I was there for a scheduled meeting, but what did I know, thinking, ok, I guess that's the price of doing airline business.

The receptionist told me that the Director and his staff had left for lunch and she was instructed to tell me to meet them at a nearby place called the Jade East. I found the restaurant, sat down at their table and introduced myself. The waitress came over and said everyone was having a Dingaling (double Bloody Mary), so wanting to fit in, I ordered the same. The first thing the Director said to me was "fasten your seat belt, you have a tough job in front of you". Once again I responded…" if it's on a blueprint, I can fix it"!

That night I was at the hanger for the midnight shift to meet the staff and the Lead Man of the shift. One of the workers told me that he was around somewhere. While I was waiting for him, I decided to check things out on my own and walked around this state of the art cargo complex. Needing to use the men's room, I walked into the lavatory and there I stumbled on the Lead Man with one of the women workers engaged in a compromising position. I was somewhat embarrassed, and said "sorry to bother you guys, I see your system is obviously in working order but we have to meet right now regarding the automatic cargo system problem".

He was not the greatest of help, since when I asked him why the system did not perform and was out of service…his only response was "we need to buy a new machine".

After his intelligent response, my next step was to review the maintenance records and then watch the operation myself. The machine operated automatically retrieving items from bins, then delivering them to a tow line of carts for the truck dock. The problem that was occurring was that many times the machines were going to empty bins, this resulted in damage to the overall system.

The first thought I had was that maybe this was more of a human problem than a mechanical one. So, I installed a 24 hour guard on each machine. Much to everyone's surprise, the machines worked 24/7 without a breakdown.

It turned out that some workers were erasing the master commands from the machine's logic box and then placing bets among themselves on which cargo bin the machine would destroy.

Once the system was proven successful, the airline was elated and not only did I sign an ongoing contract with the provider, but also as a result, it provided me with additional assignments.

I found this airline business fascinating...each day representing a new and different challenge.

There was a sense of excitement and I, like my colleagues, became a JFK junkie. I was addicted.......the airline business got me! There was no turning back.

AIRLINE ADDICTION CONTINUED

By John Mangano

Following my success in solving the problem with the automatic cargo system, my next assignment was to oversee the busing of airline employees to and from their parking lot, to the International Arrivals Building (IAB). This may sound simple, but the logistics involved with scheduling drivers and setting up the necessary maintenance to keep sixteen buses operating around the clock, made it a challenging job.

One incident stands out…we had several breakdowns of the buses and in addition, an undue number of drivers were out sick. This resulted in long delays as the airline employees had to wait for extended periods to get to their jobs at the IAB. Frustration finally boiled over when one individual took matters into his own hands. He climbed aboard a bus that was sitting there with no driver, got behind the wheel, loaded the bus up with other waiting employees and drove it on his own to the terminal.

He pulled up to the front entrance, parked it, walked inside to his job and then called us to come pick up the "stolen" bus.

Now a Manager at the airport…to this day, he is known as the Jackie Gleason (aka Ralph Cramden of the Honeymooners) bus robber of JFK.

Just another day at the airport, you never know what is going to happen next! One thing you can always count on however, whatever does happen will be unexpected!

Just such an unexpected event occurred when the Concord SST first began flying into JFK. The airline scheduled a press conference to promote the start of SST service.

The Airline Manager was tasked with developing a plan to move the Concord from the tarmac over to the hanger where the press conference was going to be held. His plan included the provision that no one but the service team of cleaners would be the only people allowed to be on the aircraft while it was being towed over to the hanger. However, he could not resist the temptation to ride along himself. His plan also included having a stair truck meet the Concord at the hanger so he could deplane, since he was also in charge of the press conference.

As the plane reached the hanger, the Port Authority Police took over control and for security reasons decided to lock down the aircraft and not let anyone off. Of course, the schmuck missed his own press conference!

JFK is not the only airport where the unexpected happens, it's endemic to the airline industry worldwide.

It was the end of the day on a Friday when my Duty Manager came into my office and asked me when I had last spoken to the head of our operation at Boston's Logan Airport. I said "today during our regular morning conference call".

He told me that he had just gotten off the phone with him and he was involved in an incident with a police car as he was heading home after a few drinks at the Cloud Nine Lounge in Boston's Logan Airport.

I immediately placed the call. He got on the phone and explained that he was driving home in his company car when the car in front of him (the police car) stopped and he hit it. I told him I would catch a flight from LaGuardia to Logan and he immediately asked if I was coming up to fire him? I told him "no, but that I needed to hold a company hearing to determine all the facts about the incident".

I took the Eastern Airlines Shuttle to Boston on Sunday at 6PM…believe it or not he called every hour all weekend long asking again and again if I was coming up to fire him.

He was at the gate to meet me when the flight landed and I assumed he would take me to a hotel for the evening. The first words out of his mouth were "are you here to fire me"? I once again assured him that we needed to have a company hearing before any action was taken. He then proceeded to tell me that he had not secured a hotel for me and that he was taking me to his house for dinner with he and his wife and also to sleep over.

His wife greeted me at the door and the first words out of her mouth were "are you going to fire my husband for hitting the police car with a baseball bat"?

She had spilled the "Boston Beans"…he not only hit the police car with our company car, he then proceeded to get out of the car and smash it with a baseball bat for getting in his way…I guess he may have had more than one or two cocktails at the Cloud Nine!

Fortunately for him, since he was well acquainted with the police, the charges were subsequently dropped. However, our company could not condone that type of behavior, so we were forced to let him go.

Eventually, he learned to control his bat swinging activities, formed his own airline service company, got a lucrative contract from Delta Airlines, and made a small fortune. He is now happily retired.

As I said, you never know what to expect in the airline business except the unexpected!

FOR THE EVIL LOVE OF MONEY
Anonymous

Working at JFK Airport was an unbelievable experience for a dear friend who shared the below story with me for Tales From The Tarmac. For him, the airport was a wonderful way to experience the various cultures and individuals who worked there. We can all agree that it takes a certain type of person to handle an airport environment, one that is eager never to have two days alike.

One night while working late at the IAT, in the blink of an eye, the place was swarming with FBI and other law enforcing agencies. Being engrossed in his work, he had no idea what had happened. He disclosed the following events based on the information that was given to him that night. It is a story of how *insane* human beings can be, if they are desperate enough for money.

A female pax came in on a flight from the Caribbean and she had a baby with her that she claimed was not feeling well. While airborne, the f/a's noticed that the baby did not move during the entire flight. Once the passenger deplaned, the flight attendant alerted the Customs and Immigration officers of her suspicions that something was amiss during her in-flight observation of the woman and her baby.

To act on the flight attendant's diligence, when the woman was going through immigration, the astute INS officer kept asking her for additional documents so that he could take a look at the baby that she was carrying in her arms. This forced her to reach into her pocketbook and fumble around long enough for the officer to focus on the baby.

Being aware of the situation, another immigration officer came from behind her and asked if she needed help. When he offered to hold the baby, the fear in her voice was evident as she quickly responded "NO"! As she tried to abruptly move away from this officer, the baby's head fell to the side and both officers realized the baby was as white as a ghost. Immediately, they asked her to hand over the baby to them and she panicked and was subsequently arrested.

Based on the autopsy report, the gruesome cause of death was murder. That innocent little infant, approximately eight months old was intentionally killed just prior to the flight and stuffed with drugs. The woman was fully aware of this atrocity.

This story is still so inconceivable, to know that a human being is capable of such horrific cruelty and totally void of emotions, all ….......for the evil love of money!

A HEALTHY DISREGARD FOR THE IMPOSSIBLE
By Henk Guitjens

How to make money when the world is on fire!

- August 2, 1990, Iraq invades Kuwait and seizes the oil fields
- August 6, UN imposes a trade embargo on Iraq
- August 7, Saudi Arabia requests U.S troops to defend them against a possible Iraqi attack
- August 9, First U.S military force arrives in Saudi Arabia
- August 10, Saddam Hussein declares a "jihad" or holy war against the U.S and Israel
- Sept 14-15, U.K and France announce deployment of 10,000 troops to the Gulf
- Jan 12, 1991. Congress grants President Bush the authority to wage war
- Jan 17, Operation Desert Storm begins at 3 a.m., Baghdad time.

On January 17, 1991, while attending a function at the Netherland Club in NYC at Rockefeller Centre, the reception came to a halt around 7 p. m. when the news broke that the US declared war on Iraq and that an invasion would be imminent. As we were watching the news with our mouths open, we wondered what this would mean for the economy - the business at hand and for our future.

As VP and GM for Martinair Holland (MP), we were knee-deep in the process of launching a substantial charter and scheduled charter program from Amsterdam to multiple cities in the United States and Canada. Programs were printed and agreements were made with the consolidators and the travel industry. The sales staff was busy selling the seats to the travel agents and an advertising campaign had started. In 1991, Martinair was operating a convertible fleet with DC-10s and 747,s.

As the cargo market historically always was stronger during the winter season, most of the aircraft were converted into a cargo configuration, whereas in the spring and the summer, passenger seats replaced the cargo floor. As per the planning, all Martinair's cargo aircraft would be converted in April 1991.

One can imagine when I returned to the office the next day; our staff was quite worried about this sudden development. The news channels were reporting on the imminent invasion and the papers were full with the troop's deployments. The public, understandably, was becoming very concerned about this development and soon it became clear that many of them wanted to stay close to home.

Passengers began canceling their reservations, groups were canceled and the business traveler was holding back their plans to travel. Any new bookings had stopped and the consolidators and tour operators were approaching MP to reduce the allotments.

One morning, at the end of January, my phone rang and the president's executive secretary said, "Henk 'the Boss' wants you to be at HDQ at Schiphol by tomorrow". That night, I climbed on KL644 and flew to Amsterdam. Other area managers of Martinair were called in as well.

After freshening up upon my arrival in Amsterdam, the meeting with Martin Schroder and his executive staff commenced. He looked all of us in the eye and said, "I am canceling the North American passenger program, except for Florida and the Caribbean, and I am converting the fl eet into cargo!"

Then he said: "Guitjens, I want to fly for the US Government! I know that they will require a lot of cargo lift and I do not believe that the U.S. carriers can supply enough airplanes". To which I said: "Martin, that will be difficult to do, as we are not a U.S. carrier and we are not part of the **CRAF** (Civil Reserve Air Fleet) program".

Martin Schroder said: "I really do not care, go to the Pentagon, the State Department, call the Dutch Ambassador in Washington, go to the **MAC** (Military Air Command) and get it done!"

He assigned the VP of International Affairs to the team and we started to plan a visit to the various U.S. government departments. After several days, we were able to establish appointments in Washington and Scott Air Force base. After speaking to them, we quickly learned from MAC that many U.S. carriers could not supply enough airplane lift and MAC was looking for a way to approach their allies and the European and Asian carriers.

In the meantime, we did a "dog and pony" show in the USA as we spoke to several Generals and Colonels at the Pentagon and Scott Air Force base, trying to convince them to consider MP's cargo fleet. It was never done before and there appeared to be great concern about a reaction by Congress, the complicated **CRAF** prerequisites, and by the U.S. carriers and their unions.

But MP had taken the initiative and **MAC** became interested in talking to us. They quickly dispatched a team to Holland and visited KLM and MP (KLM at that time owned 50% of Martinair). They discussed the fleet of Martinair, looked at the financial records, the maintenance programs and viewed the regulatory process.

MAC realized that MP could supply the additional lift and was a very reliable company. Our maintenance records were excellent and better yet, MP owned American manufactured planes. Yet there was another complication, which was that it was difficult for the U.S. Government to dispatch funds and payments to a foreign carrier. Also, there was not enough time to obtain waivers or permission since supplies and troops had to be moved quickly.

The payment issue was resolved whereby monetary donations of a foreign government could be applied for payment. Hence, it became a tripartite arrangement. MP could fly the cargo missions, the U.S. Government had made the agreement and another government would make the payments to MP. In addition, the U.S. Government took over the war-risk insurance, and guaranteed the fuel supply.

When all the parties agreed, contracts were signed and MP started flying for the U.S. Government. It was mostly "sustainment goods" or cargo, as it was called, and about 100 missions were flown from various U.S. Air Force bases to Germany and to the Middle East. At the same time the U.S. Government used the Rotterdam harbor to bring large amount of troops to Europe by naval ships. MP was hired to supply the catering upon arrival before the troops were dispatched by rail to Germany and flown to the Middle East.

It was a major effort by the MP's staff, inspired by MP's President and founder Martin Schroder, who never took **"no"** for answer. Martin Schroder always had a *"healthy disregard for the impossible"*.

The 1991 Martinair's annual report shows a FL75* Million gross profit and a FL52 Million net profit, an increase of 83% over the year 1990. The flexibility, the vision of Martin Schroder and his staff and adequately taking advantage of the changes in the world arena, has always served Martinair well.

*FL (Dutch guilders)
November 19, 2010 Rev: 4

TAIL "IN" THE TARMAC
By Timber, (T.R., T-Man)

Due to the political turmoil in Iran both then and now, literary anonymity was requested by an endearing friend who graciously offered to share with us events in his life that warrant concealing his identity. For the following three amazing stories, he shall respectfully be referred to as "Timber", T-man, or simply TR. He is however, the antithesis of simplicity.

Circa 1957-1982

Timber was a Lieutenant Colonel and pilot instructor in the Iranian Imperial Air Force. In 1971, he was stationed in Hamadan Air Force base in western Iran, before being deployed as a fighter pilot in the F5 to Vahtaati Air Force base in Southern Iran, due to the conflict within Iraq. Northern Iran's climate and topography was cold and mountainous, however, Vahtaati AFB was located in the sweltering desert. Flights were scheduled in the evening because of the intense heat and sand storms with temps averaging 120 degrees. This wreaked havoc on the pilots and the a/c's since this particular AFB had no hangers for the F5's. Every two hours the pilots, in 'full flight" equipment had to do cockpit rotations due to the intense heat and to avert heat strokes while sitting in the cockpit, they had to continuously pour cold water on their oxygen masks.

One evening Timber received a "Scramble Line" (priority in aircraft take-off) from the tower to scramble out at 7:30 **URGENT.** As a result of the two hour rotation, on this particular flight, Timber was the #2 wing man to the flight leader. Shortly after a "cranked out" locked formation takeoff (pedal to the metal), he started drifting back and losing speed. According to Timber, the leader requested that Timber go to auxiliary power and he advised that he was already on max and afterburners. He continued drifting back with the leader still ahead and quickly pulling away. He checked his instrument panel and realized the right engine wasn't putting out enough power. The leader said he'd follow him back and instructed him to bank left, circle and start the descend. TR then made a shallow turn to land and maintained an altitude of 300 ft.

With much anguish, he put his landing gear down for final approach and the a/c began dropping at an alarming speed. In such cases, instrumentation and flight controls work in reverse…ARC, area of reversed command. At only 40 rpm's, he calmly but desperately tried to restart the right failing engine. At zero power, it had completely shut down at which point, the tower advised him to eject **NOW!**

Life or death situations are predicated on split second avionic judgment calls on the ground or in the air with very little time to pray for divine intervention. With his life hanging in the balance, he had to make one of those life altering nano- second judgment calls….i.e…to bail or not to bail.

True to form, the Iranian Indiana Jones chose the latter, for two logical reasons. One being, that he felt a sense of loyalty to try and save the a/c and the other was the fact that he was very frightened about ejecting because he knew the problems many pilots had encountered with the ejection seat on that jet fighter. There were reported incidents by his NATO F5 pilot colleagues where ejection seats had malfunctioned. The manufacturer, which we all know, but I was asked not to divulge, refused to acknowledge the harrowing defects. As a result, many pilots were killed or crippled.

The ejection seat mechanisms on the F5 caused instant death because the breakthrough canopy device was located on the top back of the seat, just behind the pilot's helmet. It was a sharp spike with a point on top of it that purposely shattered the canopy so the seat could eject. The device would embed itself into the pilots spine by going downward in lieu of upward. Horrific scenarios flashed through his mind, to either eject with the probability of being a vegetable in a wheelchair or die should it malfunction. For TR, both would have been a death sentence, *or* to hold on tight to the stick, and brace for impact. There was no choosing the lesser of two evils because both options sucked. True to form, TR braced himself, held on for dear life and crashed his F5 on final approach at a speed of 135 knots an hour. Upon the initial impact, the a/c broke into three sections as it hit the ground with the nose up. The nose which contained the ammunition (50 caliber rounds)) and oxygen apparatus immediately caught on fire in front of him. He could hear the ammunition detonating only fifteen feet away as he sat trapped in the cockpit. The tail which contained the fuel broke off ten feet behind him. While still harnessed in the pilot's seat, he was saturated with fuel when the seat started tilting right on a 90 degree angle. His left leg got stuck in a hole on the tarmac that was made when he crashed. As a result, his leg stayed in place while the seat and his trapped and bloody body keeled over. The visual is analogous to a mighty tree toppling over while the root remains firmly planted in the ground, hence the nickname TIMBER. He vividly remembers the sound of all the bones in his limb being pulled in half and shattering while being drenched in fuel with the nose fifteen feet away still ablaze. He attributes the tail not exploding due to extreme crosswinds which blew the fumes away from the cockpit. He laughed when he said, "boy, I was lucky. I would have been shish kebob on a six foot skewer. It was really hot, TR said nonchalantly and then I lost consciousness".

He had no recollection of the rescue, only what he was told by the ground crew who saved his life. Since Timber crashed only ten feet short of the runway, it enabled them to rescue him immediately. The crew used a ladder to pull him out of the cockpit and improvised by using it as a stretcher. They also told him that when he was placed on the ladder, his entire left leg was dangling in mid air and hanging by a thread.

The AFB hospital was only half a mile away from the crash site. Due to the highly trained rescue efforts of the ground crew, TR had regained consciousness despite his burns and agonizing injuries and while in the emergency room, his maverick mindset was intact and he found it quite amusing that the young macho doctor on duty that night was watching The Sound of Music in the AFB theater. The Julie Andrews groupie was astonished when he saw Timber's severely mangled body and immediately called for a back up of five additional surgeons. The shoulder harness on the ejection seat had cut so deeply into his shoulder and neck, that the doctor felt he would die due to total blood loss. The Sound of Music enthusiast and his team did prevent TR from bleeding to death by aggressively stitching up most of his neck and right shoulder. One month later he was released from the hospital never to be the same again.

The debilitating pain, wounds and permanent scars did not slow him down any longer than necessary. As a true aviator, Timber bit that bullet, spread his wings and once again took his rightful place in the esteemed "first" seat!

THE ONE AND ONLY
By Timber, (T.R., T-Man)

From 1978 to 1982, our man Timber was the Pahlavi Imperial family's (Shah of Iran) personal 747 pilot. Among the Shah's many opulent spending sprees under the guise of national security, he had purchased sophisticated radar equipment from a well known U.S. electronic firm which I was asked not to disclose. The Shah requested to have this equipment flown directly from the U.S. to Iran without it being public knowledge. In order to do so, he purchased several used 747's from TWA and had them converted strictly to carry cargo. Boeing was most happy to accommodate the Shah, since as Timber regaled, "Boeing was discreetly paid astronomical figures in good old U.S. Dollars. However, despite his wealth and purchasing power, the Shah faced a major "air-time" impediment tantamount to Newton's first law of motion, what goes up, must come down....and in this situation, sooner than later! TWA arranged clandestine monetary rendezvous' with his royal highness, Mr. Pahlavi. The truism that money talks and bullshit walks is not just a euphemism, it is simply politics at its every day core level.

McGuire Air Force Base in New Jersey to Tehran was twelve hours of actual flight time. The Shah's request to reconfigure the a/c from pax to cargo dropped the fuel weight to increase the cargo capacity which further limited the 747's performance. Even with a max fuel load i.e....total fuel consumption for taxing, take-off, in-flight, holding and landing etc., the 747 was three hours short. Just to reach a cruising altitude of 33,000 ft., this a/c required sixty thousand pounds of fuel. So in order to fly non-stop MAFB/Tehran, a solution to the three hour flight time shortage had to be found. The one and only answer was in-flight refueling.

Amir Fazli was a lieutenant general commander at the Air Force Base in Tehran. This was the only person's name that Timber disclosed in his compendium of "Tales From The Tarmac". I asked him why, to which he nonchalantly responded..."he's fucking dead"! He felt all the other prominent individuals in his tales except Fazli and the Shah, should remain anonymous along with his own identity for fear of political and criminal reprisal. The Shah was aeronautically astute since he had been a seasoned pilot himself and owned a fleet of private a/c's. The two men had a good rapport. Timber not only flew the royal family around on their decadent imperial 747, but as a personal favor to the Shah, he trained Pahlavi's son to fly during his tour of duty in the imperial air force.

General Fazli knew that Timber's avionic efficacy was just what the Shah needed to resolve the McGuire/Tehran long-range fuel shortage dilemma, unlike my daily dilemma of what to feed our two feral cats.... soft or dry cat food! Th ere was only one man for the job, T-Man! He would be the first pilot in aviation history to refuel a 747 mid air. This became known as the Tanker/Receiver Project.

Subsequently, Timber was sent to JFK for six months where he attended TWA's flight training school via the simulator which was his first introduction to flying the 747 all-cargo a/c. There were a few snags of course that Timber had to contend with. Since the a/c's had been purchased by the Shah, they were the property of Iran, but they flew under TWA's flag to conceal the covert operation. To deter any suspicion he had to wear the TWA flight uniform. He laughed while telling us this story because the in-flight crews really took a liking to Timber but would always ask him, are you an *A*raab? He was a young good looking stud (and still is) with a demeanor and profile of an Iranian Indiana Jones. He was eye candy for the 747 stews (former nickname for flight attendants). It was fun watching Timber's facial expressions as he humbly regaled "they all wanted a part of me and a good time was had by all....a *really really* good time"! No one expected such a young hottie to be flying a 747 which was the purview of older geriatric 747 pilots. After completing his JFK training, Timber was sent to Seattle for more intensive training where he eventually got his tanker/receiver certification. He then returned to Tehran to train Iranian 747 pilots to refuel mid air.

Not knowing that the Shah owned the TWA 747's and based on an in-depth cost analysis study, the US Gov't. determined that utilizing 747's for this project was not monetarily feasible and they felt using smaller a/c's to accomplish the same goal would be more cost effective. However, the Shah clearly insisted on the 747 since its long-range cargo capability was the reason he purchased them in the first place. He also knew that the 747 was at that time, the fastest subsonic cargo a/c on the earth at mach .92 at a normal cruising speed. Once again, the dollar spoke even louder than before since the Shah was not going to scrap the project after already paying for all the radar equipment, the 747's and training, etc. Magically, the U.S. Gov't agreed.... contingent on the Shah footing the bill with crispy green "cash only" instructions. Obscene amounts of cash were flown into the U.S. from the Pahlavi's endless fortune and as per instructions from the imperial palace, Timber had to deeply line greedy pockets and heavily grease outstretched palms.

The one and only actual 747 refueling began over Nantucket, Mass, when he was 45 minutes airborne at 22,000 ft. A **KC135** tanker a/c belonging to the USAF hovered fifteen ft. above his 747, ten ft. from the tail. T-man said, he could see the whites of the KC crewmen's eyes. A solid flexible hose locked into the nose of the 747 from the KC tail and the successful refueling took thirty minutes. A boom operator is the tech man o/b the KC that deploys the boom (hose) out of the rear of the KC tanker a/c. He negotiates the actual transfer from the KC to the 747, aka male/female receptor. Upon completion of the fuel transfer, the KC disconnects and the 747 then flies to its cruising altitude. Timber laughed when he said, during the refueling, he and everyone smoked their cigarettes. The refueling process repeated again in Spain via another USAF jet. Again after thirty minutes at 22,000 ft., Timber cruised back up to 39,000 and headed home to the Shah's kingdom. Total flight time from From McGuire AFB in New Jersey to Tehran, was thirteen and a half hours. Upon landing in Tehran, all the engine lights were illuminated like a Christmas tree. This 747 cargo a/c's oil usage could not exceed eleven hours of flight time, but this time it did. Since only fuel could be replenished mid air and not oil, it was a no-go for any future tanker/receiver flights. The USAF canceled its commitment labeling the reason: "sensitive needs of the 747 oil usage". In essence, all the money that was spent on this project simply *tanked* (pardon the pun) and went down the tubes. I do not profess any sympathy for the royal family losing billions of dollars since it was literally only pocket money and a mere spit in the ocean for them anyway. Eventually Pratt & Whitney and Boeing modified the a/c's by making them shorter and faster using less fuel and oil.

Timber was and still is a unique character that does not command respect, he simply deserves it and has certainly earned mine!

"EGGS"ODUS
By Timber, (T.R., T-Man)

Home is where the heart is, so they say, but at what price? TR loved his country as any good citizen does, regardless of the corruption in leadership. His childhood memories of his close-knit family that had lived in Iran for generations were loving. However, what he proudly considered as a beloved homeland became one of imprisonment and punishment. In the latter part of 1982, three years after Deb and the children left, he made a most difficult decision, to flee Iran knowing he could never return. He knew the dangers involved if he were to be caught, but the risk factors at that point of his life were secondary. Had TR been captured, he surely would have had a backup plan since his attitude was...there are more ways than one to skin a cat. After careful plotting, he seized the moment when the opportunity presented itself.

Empress Farah Pahlavi, (Shah's wife) frequently went on shopping sprees via one of their imperial toys, the 747 that was at her beckoned call, along with Timber. It was nothing unusual for him to fly all over the world for the Pahlavi's nonsensical whims. One day, he received orders from the imperial air force to fly to Paris for Mrs. P. to pick up curtains that she ordered. As absurd as it sounds to us, it was par for the course for her. Tehran to Paris roundtrip was approx. ten hours of flight time. The costs incurred for such trips were ludicrous. In addition to fuel, landing fees had to be paid as well. Each time, TR underhandedly had to dish out $2000 USD and pay bribes on the tarmac so he could just walk into ops, get his manifest and fly right back out. On this particular trip as he picked up the cargo manifest and read CURTAINS and a pair of BOOTS for the empress, the insanity had reached its peak. Shortly after that shoe flight, the Shah and his family were ousted from Iran by the Islamic revolutionaries and exiled to the U.S.

Life, as Iranians knew it under the Shah's regime was a dichotomy. There was terrorism, but not blatant, there was wealth, but not apportioned. Having dual citizenship was normal and people were free to come and go. Women were not mandated to veil their faces and drape their bodies in public. Socio-economically, the Shah did much good for Iran's infra-structure. The Pahlavi's mindset was more secular as opposed to the fanatical theocracy that killed innocent people since the beginning of time. Many friends like Deb and TR, as well as my sister Edith and my nephew Kevan lived in Tehran for many years during the Shah's rule and also under the equally as corrupt Khomeini regime. My family was empowered monetarily and socially but that ended immediately after the Shah was overthrown. Everyone's life changed for the worse, yet the worst *was* and *is* still to come.

For TR, it was time to flee! After the terrible transition, the Khomeini revolutionary guards ordered Timber to pick up eggs in Amsterdam....and not for breakfast mind you. His missions on the 747 were to pick up 130 TONS of eggs per day for seventeen consecutive days under the pretense of feeding the nation that the shah had impoverished. Other flights on a 707 flew from Tehran to Paris every day for beef. Nothing much phased TR any more because of all the craziness he had witnessed. However, he was thoroughly shocked when he saw that the daily palates containing the 130 tons of eggs at Amsterdam's Schiphol Airport came from Israel via EL AL airlines. As he so bluntly put it...."how about that ...Jewish eggs feeding Iranian revolutionaries, 'ya gotta love it". Just prior to his fourteenth egg flight, an Intel Officer who was a friend and an informant, told TR that the mullah's were getting into his files. The same mullah's had already killed several of TR's colleagues, so he had to be extremely discreet in his stealth-like escape that would take place within a few hours.

TR's First Officer on that fourteenth egg-run flight was a loyal Khomeini follower who was assigned to surreptitiously observe him. TR had already checked out the info he needed during the pre-flight re: weather etc.. He knew he had to remain cool as a cucumber in that cockpit to stay alive and carry out his plan. While airborne, he calmly told the sycophant (Khomeini ass kisser) F/O to fi le an alternate flight plan for Frankfurt, Germany just in case the weather conditions in Amsterdam for landing were too severe. **ATIS**, (air terminal ident services) comparable to our **NOTAMS**, was a radio frequency in the cockpit for landing information. TR told them he opted to bring the aircraft down in Frankfurt due to the heavy rainstorms in Amsterdam. ATIS clearly advised him that Frankfurt airport had an equally low ceiling. When the F/O realized TR was heading for the runway in Frankfurt, he said to him "what the *hell* are you doing"? TR quietly landed and parked the 747 out on the tarmac and once again cool as a cucumber he walked out of the a/c and inwardly cried **free, I'm free, just keep walking. Don't look back!** He was honorable enough to walk into ops and order an alternate captain. He left his cherished homeland with a calloused heart, the flight suit he had on his back, his standard flight bag and $500.00 in his pocket which was all he was allowed to take on any given trip. The next day TR went to the American consulate under "emergency" circumstances to come to the states. At that time, Russia was fighting in Afghanistan and as a result many Afghani's tried to flee to the U.S.. President Carter mandated that anyone trying to come here, irregardless of their country, had to be cleared by the State Dept., otherwise it was a no-go. He pleaded his case stating that his wife and children were already in the U.S. He certainly could not tell them that twenty four hours ago, he absconded from Iran. They told him to keep checking back intermittently should there be any new State Dept. directives, however, no one gave him a time frame. TR now faced yet another challenge....where to go. He knew he had to go into hiding and that he had to count every penny since there was uncertainty as to how long he would be forced to remain underground. He discarded his Iranian flight suit and somehow had to procure money to buy clothes and to pay off people who could potentially help him secure passage to the U.S. That was his priority.. He was cold, he was hungry, he was alone, he was homeless. There was no longer an Iran to which he could profess allegiance as he had done all his life. He recalled eating only Bratwurst on a stick a couple of times a day from street vendors since that was all he could afford. One of those bratwurst encounters paid off!

TR had just finished his meager meal while sitting on a set of cement steps in front of a building when a stranger sat next to him having a quick lunch on the go. The polite man struck up a conversation with TR and he introduced himself as a doctor who worked in a local Frankfurt hospital. They conversed in English and in the course of conversation, the doctor came to realize that TR spoke Farsi (Persian). This impromptu meeting was a stroke of luck for TR after forty five days in hiding. The doctor told TR that a patient of his needed someone to translate from Farsi to English since neither one spoke the other's native language. The doctor was most willing to pay someone handsomely for their services and up until that point, he had not found anyone who would go to the hospital, sit and translate. TR hesitated, but finally agreed knowing that would be his ticket out of Germany, one way or another. They arranged to meet shortly afterward in the patient's room and once again TR had to crank up the old "cool as a cucumber" routine when the alarming introduction was made.

The patient was an acute opium/heroine addict who had serious drug and legal entanglements with the law as a result of his severe addictions. TR said his wife would sneak huge amounts of opium into his room and he'd smoke it all in a heartbeat. When she was forbidden to carry anything in to him, out of desperation, the junkie begged the doctor to roll some dope up in cigarettes and he'd be generously rewarded. Needless to say, the answer was NO. TR was not really surprised about the lowlife condition of the addict, since opium grows wild all over Iran. As my sister once said, it grows like crabgrass, through cracks in cement sidewalks. The shocker for TR was not this man's addiction, but rather who he was. TR's life once again flashed in front of him with an overwhelming threat of being captured, after he'd come so far from oppression and so close to freedom. This despicable addict was a Khomeini bodyguard and close relative of Khomeini's secretary of agriculture. Fortunately, TR never disclosed anything about himself after the Shah's exile, nor did he do so in Frankfurt. He took the money owed him by the doctor and politely said *aufwiedersehn* Herr Doktor!

With money in his empty pockets, TR went back to the consulate two months later and showed that he could pay for a ticket. The consulate approved and issued him a travel voucher which had to be presented at the airport upon check-in. He humbly requested an ID90 (industry discount 10% fare) from Lufthansa to JFK. TR laughed as he slowly elongated the words "I had one skinny shiny dime in my pocket by the time I got to Atlanta." When the a/c left Frankfurt and started climbing, he asked for a cup of tea. He calmly sipped it while doing mental and emotional housecleaning. Some things he saved, while other things had to be discarded like painful shoes that were loved, but just kept hurting! Inwardly TR was a softie! As his profound existence in Iran ended, his new life was soon to begin. Humbly he whispered "I knew freedom was only eight hours away"!

FAREWELL TO ARMS
By Debbie R.

Hemingway's classic novel, *A Farewell To Arms*, symbolically portrays the vicissitudes of life for one couple's journey during WW11. The good/bad, safety/danger, chaos/calm are only a few of the paradoxes in which the world must function. Had Hemingway had the opportunity to meet my friend Debbie, he would surely have immortalized her in one of his novels.

Debbie and I go back to the mid 60's. We were both dancers in a Ukrainian Folk dance troupe where ethnicity was a prerequisite. Her Ukrainian/Italian upbringing afforded her cultural opportunities at home in good old Brooklyn and abroad. Intellectually, she was highly sought after in her profession with her name topping many headhunters priority lists. She was the recipient of numerous prestigious awards and positions in the educational field. Her list of accomplishments are astounding. Today she has a thriving psychology practice and is the dean of a university in Georgia.

In 1969, Debbie answered an ad in New York for a lucrative position as a computer programmer in downtown Tehran. This position was unheard of for a woman, especially an American woman. After the details were agreed upon, along with her passion for travel and adventure, she accepted the job and moved to Iran. She had been romantically involved with a young Iranian man whom she married. Her adaptability and fondness for the culture, the language etc. lasted, but the marriage did not. Subsequently a year later she returned to visit her parents in New York, but was beckoned back to Iran at the request of the Iranian Ministry of Water & Power (her former employer) who graciously financed her return trip.

Since Debbie's former husband had been in the Iranian Navy, when she traveled, she flew via military equipment. One day while waiting for a flight at the base, she met a dashing gentleman. He was a handsome C130 pilot, with a smile and a personality that sparked her interest.

Having respect for destiny, they both ensued a long distance relationship. Deb and the senior officer in the Imperial Iranian Air Force, none other than T-man, were eventually married in Iran. Being atypical newlyweds, Deb felt the only way for them to remain attached at the hip would be for her to secure employment at the base. Deb knew that teaching jobs were readily available. With a scholastic background in education, she applied and was trained by the U.S. Dept. of Defense language school. Then, when T-man got transferred to Shiraz, south of Tehran, the general at the AFB asked her to open an ESL (English as a second language) school on base.

In the late 70's, political and civil unrest ensued with subsequent danger to Americans living in Tehran, especially to wives of Iranian officers. This forced Deb and T-man to plan an exit strategy. T-man suggested that she take herself and their children to the U.S. and live with her parents until he himself could execute a plan to flee. As difficult as it was, they both knew it was in their best interest and safety.

Aliens and nationals up until that point always had the freedom to travel. Many people had dual citizenship with Iran and their respective secondary countries. As a result of the tyrannical Khomeini takeover, it was very dangerous to leave Iran and to get through customs with an American passport. American women that were married to Iranian nationals were automatically deemed Iranian citizens, therefore they could only use their Iranian passports for travel to select countries excluding the U.S. Debbie had to nonchalantly purchase roundtrip tix's to Frankfurt Germany under the guise of going on a little family vacation. From there she bought one way tix's to freedom on a KLM flight, departing Frankfurt via Amsterdam, to Tampa, Florida on November 27th, 1979.

There was much planning and rehearsing for the pending day of deception. Deb and T-man had to remain composed. The mission was to smuggle her and the children's American passports out of Iran the day she left for Frankfurt. Knowing that the revolutionists at the airport checked everything including the hems of women's clothing, their bras and carefully examined their shoes, especially boots, it was impossible to hide their U.S. Passports.

They devised the following nail-biting plan: Since T-man was a lieutenant colonel, he had access to the ramp because military and civilian a/c's shared the same tarmac. At that time, boarding a commercial a/c in Iran was accessible only via the tarmac stairs that hooked up to the a/c door. After being invasively searched, Deb remained calm and exited through customs with the children via their Iranian passports. There were no x-ray machines, only guards that would kill instantaneously on command. She had wads of money stuffed in talc powder, baby formula, baby bottles and diapers. When my sister made her daring escape from Iran, she too camouflaged money by painstakingly rolling it inside of tampons. When I asked Deb what went through her mind from the time she entered the airport until the a/c left the ground, she said "I was scared SHITLESS"!

The plan was for T-man to casually drive around the KLM a/c in a military jeep to say good-bye to his wife and children before they boarded. As Deb exited customs, she covertly looked out and did not see him. Fear and panic overwhelmed every fiber of her being yet she had no choice but to stoically keep walking and follow the crowd to the waiting a/c. As she took her first step up the stairs, she saw the jeep. Her heart raced and she calmly stepped aside to pretentiously say goodbye to him. They both knew they were carefully being watched. Due to restrictions of the Islamic revolution, neither Deb nor T-man could display public affection. It was against the law, nor could he overtly hand over their U.S. passports. The baby was in her arms with the other two children at her side. It was very cold and windy out on the tarmac that late November day and they were all bundled up. In order to get access to the passports, Deb blatantly handed the baby to T-man and told him to kiss daddy goodbye. In doing so, he took the baby out of Deb's arms, hugged him and when giving him back, he positioned his arms to envelope Deb's coat pockets. In the blink of an eye and a slight of hands, he slid the passports in her right pocket. For a brief moment, they stared at each other and silently cried. It was an internal cry of joy compounded by heartache as well, since displaying a final farewell to loving arms that held one another all those years, was strictly forbidden. All fanatical eyes were focused on Deb and TR and machine guns were ready and waiting. Neither one knew if or when they would be reunited. T-man then quietly said to her.......GO! She and the children quickly boarded and were overwrought with trepidation and sadness.

Deb retold her tale to me with such melancholy by emphasizing that pre-Khomeini Iran was a very good place to live. She had to leave a country that she comfortably called home for eleven years. Like TR and most other peaceful Iranians, they have always advocated nonviolence and love of life. They were duped into a false sense of security by the Shah's promise of democracy and westernization.....acronyms for Marie Antoinette's, let them eat cake or Nero's fiddling while Rome burnt. Eventually, the oppressed middle class became the impoverished class with loyal citizens being reduced to living in cardboard boxes outside the city limits while the Shah picked his teeth with twenty-four carat gold toothpicks.

The "freedom Movement" in the late 70's was a cry for equality, to respect the original constitution of 1906 which the shah disregarded. Unbeknownst to the innocent Iranians, they traded a perversed monarchy for a maniacal theocracy hoping to replace the Shah's secular greed with spiritual leadership. It SO backfired. As Debbie said, the peaceful mindset of most Iranians today is the same as it was back then. The fundamental difference between then and now is that Islamic revolutionists have become even more hateful, not just in Iran, but worldwide.

When Deb landed in Frankfurt, remnants of Octoberfest were still in the cold windy city. The children were already missing their father. Besides keeping the children out of harm's way, physically, she had to carry the luggage, the diaper bag and the baby from the airport to downtown Frankfurt. She found innocuous accommodations in an old creeky hotel adorned with dark burgundy curtains everywhere even in the breakfast room, where a small continental breakfast unfamiliar to the children was served. Afterward, the remainder of the day was spent retrieving hidden currency in all of the different hiding places in her luggage. Trips to several banks were made in the chilling cold weather with children in tow, one of which had a fever.

This was necessary in order to exchange the variety of currencies that she smuggled out of the country.

The flight to Tampa the next day was nondescript. The children spoke frequently of "when daddy gets to America"..... and what plans they would be making for his arrival. Deb's parents waited patiently for the a/c to land in Florida. They were terribly worried about Deb and the children and rightly so. As the a/c descended upon final approach and as the tarmac was in view, the children's thoughts and memories of Iran began to fade as the excitement of landing began. Daddy would be OK...he would come soon...he promised he would! The children squealed with joy as the landing gear hit the final "bump" on the runway. One more walk...across the tarmac.....one more walk through customs....into the outstretched arms of their tear-filled grandma and grandpa. Their frightening roller coaster ride had finally come to an end, for it stopped at liberty's door...one nation under one benevolent God.

Freedom and safety are not merely privileges here in our great country, but rather birthrights to be cherished and respected. As Hemingway's WW11 couple, so too, Deb and TR survived all the emotional seasons on their journey through life. They fulfilled all their extraordinary passions with many hardships along the way. Leaving the Iran they loved and knew once upon a time was extremely difficult, but nothing was as significant as fulfilling their one last passion.....embracing liberty and justice for all!

FAST FORWARD
By Timber & Debbie R

Helen, Georgia, August 27th, 2010. Tucked in the breathtaking Blue Ridge mountains, ninety miles north of Atlanta is a little town known as Helen, Georgia. This hidden jewel is a replica of a Bavarian village in Alpine, Germany. Brightly colored gingerbread shops and houses line the cobblestone streets with locals dressed in dirndls and lederhosen year round. Who knew!

Deb and TR always dreamed of building a second getaway retirement home in the mountains after many years of hard work and sacrifice. Their dream came to fruition and after two years of contending with the proverbial builders, permits, etc., it was finally completed in June, 2010. Jack and I were honored when we were told we would be their first guests in the new house and so in August, we took a leisurely car trip to Georgia to visit with them. The house, secluded high atop a mountain was beautiful, the host and hostess were extraordinary and our time together was precious.

After dinner we would sit out on the back porch with a bottle of wine and candlelight and just experience nature at its glory. Knowing their unique history, it was the perfect time to ask favors of good friends....i.e. make literary contributions to Tales From The Tarmac. And so they graciously accommodated my intrusive questions and I began scribbling notes with only the flame of the candle as a source of light...and of course, a bottle of wine, an impertinent yet malolactic wine! As TR began reminiscing, he started laughing and said to Jack and I "do you want to touch my screws?" Now if it were anyone else, I would have taken offense to that, but we all knew what he meant. Hundreds of screws protruded through every square inch of his left leg along with massive scars from head to foot all over his fatigued body.. His pain is second nature to him as he shrugged it off so matter of factly. His wounds run deep, emotionally and physically. Deb said there isn't any one place on his body that isn't damaged. Ms. Indiana Jones also endured impassioned scarring. Her survival skills and tenacity for life itself are complimented by her genuine kindness and compassion for everyone. TR, aka Timber, aka T-man has been externally hardened by a number of life's harsh realities, yet his teddy bear demeanor are indicative of a sensitive man who was faced with moral ambiguity throughout his life. Writing a few tales about Deb and TR do not do them justice. Perhaps my next project, should this one succeed, will be to write an entire book on our Indiana Jones and our Mata Hari. It will however necessitate a longer vacation in Helen, a few more tall candles and of course, *several* bottles of the impertinent yet malolactic wine!

.....AND IN CONCLUSION.....

Almost a year after my literary journey began, I've come to the conclusion that not much has changed in the travel industry. Flights are still delayed, runways are stacked to the max with a/c's, and pax's in general still don't quite adhere to the screening drill, present company included. Granted, 9/11 deemed it a fundamental necessity but nonetheless, I somehow fail to see where a teensy tube of unopened toothpaste is cause for alarm. Yes, TSA is doing there job, but one cannot help but notice, some of the agents exude a certain sense of empowerment when they take you aside and confiscate your Revlon passion pink lip gloss, etc. What I find baffling is the fact that one agent allows six items in the little plastic baggie while another might adamantly confiscate all the extra items and yet still another agent let's you pass through with a portable amenity pantry. Why is that?

Case in point......Two years ago I had extensive oral surgeries which disabled my mandible from biting or chewing. Surgical masks (risk of infection) along with liquids or soft foods were my basic staples for well over a year until

I healed. Eventually, solid foods were back on the menu, however, cutting everything in baby pieces was par for the course. During the post-op days, when traveling was required, my routine consisted of purchasing a salad or fruit prior to boarding long-range flights. When I had the in-flight munchies, cutting the food in miniscule morsels was necessary. To resolve my onboard conundrum, I took a serrated kitchen knife from home, tightly wrapped it in aluminum foil and placed it on the bottom of my usual carry-on bag. For an entire year, the knife was undetected. I was astounded each time I walked through security, because my tiny toothpaste, my miniature mouthwash and a myriad of harmless noncombatant sundries *were* zapped, but not the knife!

Then, one sunny day at Sky Harbor airport in Phoenix, Jack and I were leaving for LGA airport via ATA. At that time, their terminal was in a little Quonset hut away from the main terminal. Totally forgetting that the knife had even been in there for so many months, I placed my bags on the belt, when one of the TSA agents finally caught the image on the screen. He took me aside and called several other agents over. Now I ask, did he *really* need back-up? That was silly! First he asked if I had a weapon in my bag.

I responded with a firm YES…. a kitchen knife that no one has detected, but yet for the past year, my little bottles of sundries were defiantly confiscated. Go figure! It was an honest assessment, but they failed to see the irony. A few more "important" people then came over and gave me several forms to fill out and they advised me these forms were going to be on file in Washington D.C. I did explain the medical reason for having it. Perhaps it was my charm that kept me out of shackles that day or simply my malleable disposition and spontaneous reaction. Whatever it was, my knife was seized, and my credibility was spared.

Passengers in general are demanding and have altruistic expectations from airline employees especially under stressful situations. On Sept. 24th, I returned back home to New York from Sacramento, Ca. via U.S. Airways. The departure time and the final destination (MacArthur airport) was convenient. In between the two coasts, I experienced a few nasty unpleasantries that were book-worthy. Upon arriving in Phoenix for my onward eastbound flight, the arrival gate was in terminal A and my connecting departure gate was in terminal F with a 35 minute window. The Sacramento a/c arrived at the gate six minutes late, leaving only a 29 minute window. Myself and the other pax's who were connecting assumed that the purser o/b would announce the gate for the connection and at very least allow us to exit the a/c first since time was of extreme essence. She did neither, nor were there any agents awaiting the a/c with gate information. With bags in tow, I sprinted and sweated through the terminals, swearing profanities under my breath at the idiot who assigned the gates. As I raced towards the departure gate totally out of breath, it was empty, with only the gate agent ready to leave the podium. The jetbridge door was closed, but it was still hooked up to the a/c. Behind me came the remaining pax's who also missed their connection.

Reggie, the US Air agent working that flight was genuinely sympathetic. I vehemently complained about the gate/distance stupidity and asked him to please call ops to let us board the flight. He made the calls, but it was an exercise in futility since the phone just rang incessantly with no response. We didn't blame Reggie. He really tried. Even as we left the gate area ten minutes later, the a/c was still hooked up to the jetbridge. Extremely upset, we all had to go the closest US Air service counter for rebooking. The agent who had the pleasure of dealing with me was a dickweed. He had no business working with distressed pax's. I once again explained the circumstances to him and he was totally indifferent and asked if I had made my reservations online. Yes,I replied. He then asked, if upon completion, I "x'ed" the US Air agreement policy on my computer. I again said yes because the screen wouldn't allow me to continue with my transaction otherwise, so I sinfully had to "x'" the box! His asinine response was "once you agree to purchase a reservation, US Air is not responsible if you miss a flight." For the third time I reiterated the 29 minute window in which I had to deplane one a/c, and race from terminal A to terminal F which in itself was a twenty minute Olympic sprint. His reply...."There's nothing I can do about it except rebook you on another flight". Already foaming at the mouth, I said ok, let's just do that. The option he gave was inconvenient, but for a fleeting moment, I begrudgingly accepted. His attitude was so offensive and I let him know. I asked for his name and he hesitated and then finally said Mark.....Mark *what* I asked....his disrespectful reply......I can't give you that. My next extremely difficult question for him was....who is the duty manager and where can I find him? His intelligent reply, while never making eye contact with me was....."I don't know". Now perhaps he was having a bad hair day, but his rudeness could not be ignored. The pax's who were standing next to me being serviced by *real* agents, came over afterward to tell me that they were appalled by Mark's attitude.

After being dismissed by him, my frustrations had reached their peak and I was determined to report that SOB to his superiors. Just then, Reggie, who was a sweetheart, saw me and came over. He sincerely apologized for everything and I asked for the manager's name etc., Reggie graciously escorted me over to him. Roy Hendricks was in the midst of handling other issues at that time and said he would be available in a few minutes. I waited near the service counter and Mr. Hendricks came over and was amenable to my plight. He escorted me to another gate, took the time to reconcile my flights, personally made hotel reservations for me in Philadelphia compliments of US Air for my layover that night and gave me a meal voucher. His professionalism, his personality and his empathy were truly impressive and genuine. I then proceeded in detail to complain about Mark and compliment Reggie.

My flight that evening to PHL was an experience I shall never forget as well. It could have been disastrous, were it not for the US Air captain whose expertise was reminiscent to Capt. Sullenberger's landing on the Hudson. Kudos to the crew on that PHX/PHL flight. Job well done!

And so, in conclusion, to all the Marks out there, I say... get a job at motor vehicles, and to all the Reggies and Roys of US Air I say...thank you kindly for your compassion and competence. And to all airline staff worldwide who have ingratiated themselves in my book and in my life, on the ground and in flight, I say with great pride and admiration....*thank you* for crossing my path!

ACKNOWLEDGMENTS

The following people have graciously taken time from their busy schedules to help fill the pages of this book. In recognition, I have also taken time to share my perception of these most interesting people and hope that I did them justice.

Lara Bozik, the kindest & greatest daughter a mother could ever wish for, with amazing inner strength that has influenced my personal growth, you gave me purpose and encouragement since the day I first held you in my arms......Former JFK airport Rep, LTU International Airways

Harry Gegner, a multi-faceted, multi-lingual no-nonsense professional.....Former KLM Lead Agent Ticket-Sales Office, Passenger Service Dept., Coordinator, Pass Bureau North America at KLM HQ

John Grasser, JFK's very own Buddy Rich, much better looking of course, a graduate of charm school and a good friend of many years......Twenty seven years with KLM Royal Dutch Airlines, working in all operational capacities culminating as Director of Stations, North America. Then for twelve years he worked in aviation roles, including security, passenger/ramspside ground handling, and terminal operations. Currently, he is Director of Airside & Baggage Operations at JFK's leading international terminal

Ursula Goeschen, a class act, true to her own beautiful self... Pan Am Coordinating supervisor, Former LTU Station Manager, Air Carnival Station Manager JFK

Henk Guitjens, a highly respected debonair intellect, a native of the Netherlands, arrived in U.S. in 1968 as Sales Manager USA Martinair Holland. He was appointed VP and GM and dubbed "Mr. Martinair". It was under his regime that Martinair became known as the "Other Dutch Airline". In 1995 he joined World Airways as Senior VP Sales & Marketing. In 1997, he was recruited by Schiphol USA and joined JFK/IAT as their VP for Airline Marketing. In 2003, he was promoted to CMO of JFK/IAT and is currently, Special Adviser to the President of JFK

Rosa Kamel, an extraordinary young lady whose wisdom far exceeds her age, and who embraces life with passion .... Former Air France Passenger Service Agent, LTU Passenger & Operations Assistant, Currently active in Real Estate

John Mangano, a man of experience, integrity, charm and compassion.....After several years of "walking steel" sixty stories in the air at the World Trade Center, he came to JFK to solve a computer cargo issue and is still there after forty years as Senior VP of Sales & Services for Triangle Aviation Services

Ann Mavroudis, Her grace, perfection and loyalty speak for themselves.... Thirty-Two memorable years with KLM, Passenger Service / Duty Manager

*Anonymity Requested.......*A benevolent friend with a heart of gold, also a brilliant Entrepreneur who has built a hugely successful business that is associated with the airline industry

Gerry Moore, The Entertainer!, a master of wit! An endearing man whose Aer Lingus career spanned from 1962 to 2001 starting with passenger service, Duty Traffic Officer, Ass't. Station Manager in Boston, Station Manager JFK, Manager for all North American Airports and culminated with VP, Customer Service, North America. In 2004, Gerry was beckoned back to JFK by Emirates. His reputation preceded him. He knew about startups, JFK airport, and most importantly, he knew the people who made JFK "work". Six years later, post-retirement, he is still managing two daily flights from Dubai ....B777 and an A380.

P.D.B, an intelligent, unpretentious wild and crazy guy, medical miracle....three time cancer survivor who remains upbeat despite his life's hurdles.....former Navy man, retired Aerospace engineer

Debbie R., a scholastic genius who sees the world through compassion, love and equality in the face of adversity...... Computer Programmer, Tehran Iran, Teacher at Iranian Air Force Bases, credited for opening several ESL schools at the AFB's, currently Associate Dean of Academic Affairs at a University in Georgia where she also has a private practice as a licensed professional counselor.

T.R./T-Man/Timber, a survivor and truly one of the most fascinating men I have ever had the privilege of knowing.... Lieutenant Colonel/ Pilot Instructor in the Iranian Imperial Air Force. Here in the U.S., he returned back to college and started a second career as a Bio-Medical Engineer. He is now literally game-fully retired, raising roosters, chickens and hens!

Dennis Wrynn, A brilliant mind, an author of various history books about WW11, and a life-long friend of my husband Jack...former TWA IAB Sales Rep, Passenger Relations Rep, Res Supervisor, City Manager for Air New England, LGA and City Manager for Ozark Airlines, LGA

Jack Oxee...WOW! You had me with... *Park Here....* and still do, not only because of your love and kindness, but your acceptance of my ubiquitous mindset....so contrary to yours! Formerly, a successful Ad-man, now semi-retired. In the summer months, Jack's favorite past-time is tweeking ticks.

To my precious granddaughter Aleah, thank you for your tarmac pix we took in Bermuda for the front cover. Who needed a graphic designer when I had you!

Special thanks to my endearing friends Linda and Jim Slezak. Jim, had it not been for your computer expertise throughout the entire year, this book would have been written on parchment paper. I owe you dear Jim, after all, one good "tern" deserves another! Dearest Linda, thank you so much for your genuine support and title contribution of "Eggs"odus in lieu of my generic title Exodus.

Ira...are you happy now! You're in! My sincere gratitude not only for your critique and your witty contribution,"Insecurity" guard, but also for your friendship dear Mendelsohns for so many beguiling years.

With Much Love and Respect to my beloved family and friends......Thank you!

NAMASTE'